ANTARCTICA

Look for these and other books in the Lucent
Exploration and Discovery series:

Australia and the Pacific Islands
The Himalayas
West Africa

EXPLORATION · AND DISCOVERY

ANTARCTICA

By Stephen Currie

LUCENT
BOOKS®

THOMSON

★

GALE

San Diego • Detroit • New York • San Francisco • Cleveland • New Haven, Conn. • Waterville, Maine • London • Munich

Jennifer Skancke, Series Editor

For more information, contact
Lucent Books
27500 Drake Rd.
Farmington Hills, MI 48331-3535
Or you can visit our Internet site at http://www.gale.com

LIBRARY OF CONGRESS CATALOGING-IN-PUBLICATION DATA

Currie, Stephen, 1960-
  Antarctica / by Stephen Currie.
    p. cm. — (Exploration and discovery)
  ISBN 1-59018-495-5
  1. Antarctica—Discovery and exploration—Juvenile literature. I. Title. II. Series.
  G863.C87 2004
  919.8'904—dc22
                                                                    2004006211

Printed in the United States of America

Foreword

For untold centuries people have wondered about the world outside their borders. The ancient Greeks imagined that a great land called Terra Incognita existed in the Southern Hemisphere. A thousand years later, medieval Europeans were captivated by the Venetian traveler Marco Polo's tales of the mountainous regions of Central Asia and China, an exotic land he called Khanbalik. The desire to know what lies beyond what we ourselves can see is an inherent part of human nature.

But more than curiosity spurred human exploration into the unknown. Historically, most expeditions across uncharted regions were launched with practical—usually financial—goals. The discovery of a new trade route or the acquisition of new land through territorial expansion was potentially very profitable for an expedition's sponsor. In the fifteenth and sixteenth centuries, an era known as the Age of Exploration, many European nations set out for new lands and new resources to increase their own wealth, power, and prestige. For example, Portuguese navigator Ferdinand Magellan sailed along the coast of South America in search of a strait that would allow him to bypass the stormy seas at the continent's southern tip en route to an important trading port in the East Indies. Finding a new sea passage would mean Portugal could import valuable Asian spices for a fraction of the cost of purchasing the prized goods from overland traders. In the mid–eighteenth century, England launched several expeditions from outposts in India into the Himalayas of Central Asia in hopes of establishing a trading relationship with Tibet that would allow the British to expand their empire around the globe.

Though the prospect of riches and territorial gain drove most organized exploration, many individuals who led such risky enterprises gained more in terms of personal glory, honor, and sense of achievement than the expeditions gained financially. Norwegian explorer Roald Amundsen, for example, won worldwide admiration when he became the first person to reach the South Pole, though there were no riches to exploit there. The sheer triumph of Edmund Hillary's and Tenzing Norgay's first successful ascent of Mount Everest evoked a sense of awe and wonder, and a shared sense of human accomplishment, from people around the world who could only imagine the view from the summit.

Humanity has derived other more tangible benefits from journeys of exploration, geographical knowledge of the world first and foremost. When James Cook ventured to the South Pacific, for example, he charted the coastlines of many remote islands and accurately measured the distances between them. In little more than eleven years, he helped fill in a portion of the map of the world that had been empty until 1760. Thanks to expeditions such as Cook's, the geographical record of the earth is nearly complete—we know the boundaries of the oceans, the routes of the safest sea passages, the contours of the coastlines, and the heights of the earth's tallest mountains.

With each exploration, humanity gains scientific knowledge as well. Sometimes discovery is entirely unexpected: For instance, in an attempt to prevent his sailors from dying on long voyages, James Cook added plenty of fresh fruit to the shipboard diet and inadvertently discovered the cure for scurvy. Sometimes scientific investigation is a secondary purpose of exploration: For example, journeys to the high peaks of the Himalayas have yielded data on the effects of altitude on the human body. And sometimes a journey's main purpose is

scientific: Deep-diving submersibles are exploring volcanoes and hydrothermal vents twenty thousand feet below the ocean surface in search of clues to the origins of life on earth. Mars rovers are equipped with sensitive instruments to detect water and other signs of life beyond our own planet. Exploration continues as humans push the boundaries in hopes of discovering more about the world and the universe.

The Exploration and Discovery series describes humanity's efforts to go to previously uncharted regions of the world, beginning with European travels and journeys of exploration, the first voyages of discovery for which abundant documentation, charts, and records have survived. Each book examines significant expeditions and voyages, highlighting the explorers—both brave and foolhardy— who journeyed into the unknown. Exciting primary-source accounts add drama and immediacy to the text, supplemented by vivid quotations from contemporary and modern historians. Each book ends with a brief discussion of the explorers' destination as it was changed by the newcomers' arrival and as it is today. Numerous maps show the explorers' routes, and abundant photographs and illustrations allow the reader to see what adventurers might have seen on reaching their destination for the very first time.

INTRODUCTION

The Bottom of the World

There is no place on earth quite like Antarctica. No other part of the world has temperatures that routinely register fifty or even a hundred degrees below zero. No other land is covered by a sheet of ice an average of eight thousand feet thick. No other continent encompasses one of the earth's poles. Antarctica has the most powerful winds, the highest average altitude, and the least precipitation of any continent. And no area of comparable size anywhere else on earth is as barren of life as is most of Antarctica.

Antarctica's terrain, location, and weather conditions have combined to make it among the least accessible places on earth. No group of people has ever settled permanently on the continent; and until very recently, the area has been completely unknown. The first people to set eyes on Antarctica did not visit the region until the early nineteenth century, and exploration of the Antarctic interior began only another hundred years after that. Of all the con-

tinents, Antarctica has been the most isolated and the most forbidding.

The Southernmost Continent

Part of Antarctica's uniqueness lies in its geography. Like Australia, alone among the other continents, Antarctica is disconnected physically from any other large landmass. While Africa and Asia, for instance, are joined to each other by a narrow strip of land, Antarctica is entirely surrounded by water. South America is the only continent that extends anywhere near Antarctica. Yet even at Cape Horn, South America's southernmost tip, the two continents are still about six hundred miles apart.

Still, the sheer distance between Antarctica and other parts of the world is not the sole reason for the continent's uniqueness. More important is Antarctica's location. Antarctica covers a rough circle around the globe's southernmost section, an area that includes the South Pole. Even the outermost stretches of the continent lie within about fifteen hundred miles of the pole. This polar location gives Antarctica two distinctive characteristics.

The first involves light and the seasons. Because of the tilt of the earth relative to the sun, the amount of daylight in the Antarctic varies considerably according to the time of year. During the Antarctic summer, which lasts from December to March, the sun never sets across much of the continent. Instead, it describes a rough circle just above the horizon. In the winter, however, the sun can go months without rising. This effect is most marked in the southernmost regions of the Antarctic. At the South Pole, in fact, the sun rises and sets just once a year.

The other result of Antarctica's polar location is the continent's climate. Antarctica is marked by bitter and almost constant cold. Temperatures as low as -129°F have been recorded in the continent's interior, and temperatures well

A harsh landscape, subzero temperatures, and a thick layer of permanent ice make the continent of Antarctica one of earth's most foreboding places.

below 0°F are common. Even during the Antarctic summer, the temperature seldom rises above freezing. The warmest part of the continent is the Antarctic Peninsula, a narrow corridor of land that snakes up toward South America. But even on this peninsula, temperatures are rarely comfortable for humans. The cold characterizes Antarctica—and to a very large extent defines it as well.

A Land of Ice

One reason for the extreme Antarctic cold is the thick layer of ice that covers virtually all of Antarctica. This ice represents the accumulation of snowfall through a period of about one hundred thousand years. Given no opportunity to melt in the bitter temperatures, the snow has become tightly compacted over time and has ultimately frozen solid. The thickness of the ice varies according to the terrain and the weather conditions, but in places, it approaches a depth of three miles. Today, between 98 and 99 percent of the Antarctic landmass is hidden under this sheet of ice.

Ice also extends into the nearby oceans. In some places around the continent's coast, the ocean has frozen into permanent sheets of ice known as ice shelves. The largest of these, the Ross Ice Shelf, lies roughly south of New Zealand. The size of the more northerly shelves may vary somewhat with the season, growing in the winter and shrinking as the Antarctic summer progresses. However, the Ross shelf and a similar one in the Weddell Sea on the other side of Antarctica are much bigger—and much less prone to shrinkage.

The total amount of ice in and around Antarctica is difficult to comprehend. Nowhere else on the globe is ice so prevalent. The Antarctic has over ten times the ice reserves contained in the frigid Arctic, for instance, and Antarctica's ice supplies dwarf those on all the mountains elsewhere in the world—combined. At least nine-tenths of the world's ice is located in and around Antarctica. These reserves account for most of the globe's total supply of freshwater as well, although because it is frozen very little of it is accessible for human use.

The ice is not merely prevalent; it is also powerful. Over the years, the growing mass of ice has changed the earth beneath it. The weight of the ice pushes down on the land and causes the continent to sink. Today, much of the land beneath the ice actually lies below sea level. And if the ice were to melt, it would have an even more powerful impact on the rest of the world. The complete melting of the Antarctic ice cap would raise the level of the world's oceans by an estimated two hundred feet, flooding low-lying countries and cities throughout the world.

The ice, in turn, makes Antarctica a difficult environment for living things. Other than bacteria, fungi, and a few other microscopic forms of life, most living things do not do well in the Antarctic. Only two species of flowering plants,

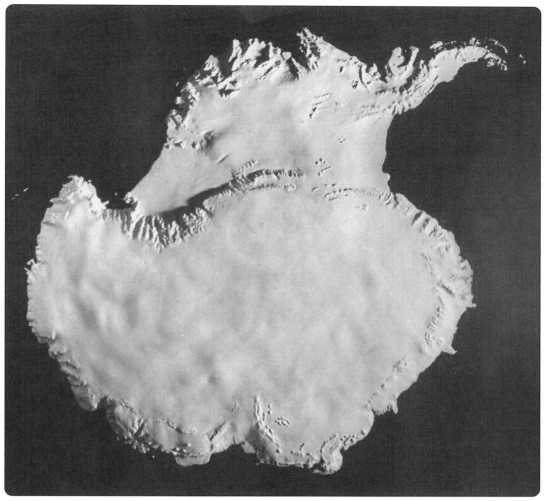

An aerial view of Antarctica reveals the landscape's barren appearance. The continent's icy environment supports only a few hardy plant and animal species.

for instance, grow anywhere on the continent; both are small and scarce, and are found only on one shore of the Antarctic Peninsula. Nonflowering plants in the region include several types of mosses and lichens. But while these plants are exceptionally hardy, even they are often frustrated by the climate: They are inactive when the weather is cold, as it usually is in the Antarctic.

Animals suffer as well. Aside from small organisms such as krill and plankton, which can be found in the oceans that surround the continent, very few large animals can thrive anywhere in the Antarctic. Several dozen types of fish make their homes in the southernmost stretches of the Antarctic oceans. Walruses, seals, and many of the world's penguin species can also be found in these waters, as well as on the ice shelves and the rocky headlands that mark the margins of the continent. But none of these creatures venture more than a short distance into the Antarctic interior. Just five or six miles from the coastline, there are few if any signs of animal life.

Antarctica and Human Exploration

If Antarctica makes survival difficult for its native plants and animals, it is far tougher for humanity. Over the years, penguins, walruses, and other living things in the Antarctic have evolved mechanisms to shut out the cold and have developed ways to find food in a harsh environment. As visitors from more temperate parts of the world, however, humans lack these advantages. Moreover, the ice, altitudes, and lack of food and shelter in the continent's interior make travel extremely difficult—and dangerous.

Yet despite the hazards and the discomforts, exploration of the bottom of the world has been an important idea throughout history. Long before anyone knew that Antarctica even existed, travelers and scientists debated what might lie at the southern end of the globe. Later explorers sought to reach the edges of the continent. And by the early 1900s,

Many of the world's penguin species make their home in Antarctica, but none are found more than a few miles from the continent's coastline.

Latitude and the Antarctic

Geographers describe locations on the earth by using two measurements: latitude and longitude. Latitude lines, sometimes called parallels, are imaginary lines that run around the surface of the earth from east to west. Longitude lines, similarly, circle the earth from north to south. Both latitude and longitude are measured in degrees. The equator, which extends around the earth's midsection, represents zero degrees. The farther a location is from the equator, the greater its measure in degrees of latitude. The South Pole, as the southernmost point in the world, lies at the maximum southerly latitude of ninety degrees south of the equator. Similar conventions determine the longitude of a point, measured according to its distance east or west of an imaginary line that runs north-south through Greenwich, England.

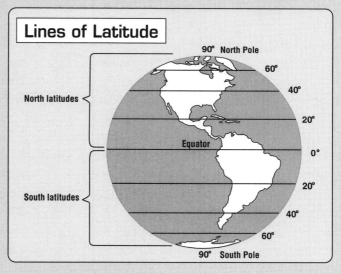

Succeeding waves of explorers, trying to penetrate farther and farther south, measured their progress by determining their latitude. Since latitude lines are imaginary and are not marked on the ground, this requires finding the distance of stars or the sun above the horizon. Modern high-tech instruments have made this an easy and straightforward process. But early explorers had to use devices such as sextants, a combination of telescope and protractor, and perform complex calculations to determine their exact position.

The concept of latitude is also useful in defining the boundaries of the Antarctic region. There are three common definitions of the Antarctic, and all three definitions have their particular uses. The most restrictive is the continent itself, along with the more or less permanent ice shelves that surround it; this can be roughly defined as the territory south of the seventieth parallel below the equator. Others define the Antarctic as the territory below a line just south of the sixty-sixth parallel, which is also known as the Antarctic Circle. And some geographers define the Antarctic as the area south of the fiftieth parallel below the equator; this definition encompasses all of Antarctica, along with a large stretch of ocean north of it.

expeditions were spending months at a time in the Antarctic and making plans to investigate the unknown interior of the continent.

Viewed one way, the exploration of Antarctica presents a puzzle. Those who made voyages of discovery to the Antarctic were giving up months, even years, of their lives in order to subject themselves to some of the most appalling hardships the earth had to offer. British explorer Apsley Cherry-Garrard entitled his memoir of an early twentieth-century Antarctic expedition *The Worst Journey in the World,* and few who visited the continent would have disagreed. Many explorers returned home from Antarctica sick or permanently injured, and several never returned at all. On one level, it seems odd that anyone would voluntarily explore such a hazardous and uncomfortable place.

But the truth is precisely the opposite. Over the years, some of the world's most dedicated and determined adventurers have been lured to the Antarctic. Among the best known of these men today are James Cook, Roald Amundsen, and Ernest Shackleton; but they are only three among many notable for their courage, leadership, and curiosity. The complications of Antarctic discovery did not keep these and other adventurers away. On the contrary, far from repelling would-be discoverers over the years, the continent's isolation and wretched conditions have actually encouraged exploration.

For an explorer, in fact, Antarctica has represented one of the greatest prizes on Earth. Throughout history, adventurers have viewed Antarctica as a supreme test of their physical, mental, and emotional strength. People who could survive in the Antarctic wastelands could say that they had experienced every peril, every misery that life had to offer—all without giving in. The push to explore the Antarctic, then, was in part a quest to prove that the human spirit was stronger than any hardships nature could offer.

CHAPTER ONE

Finding a Southern Continent

Because of its remote location and almost total inaccessibility, Antarctica was completely unknown throughout virtually all of human history. Most of the world's people, after all, lived nowhere near the Antarctic. And those who did saw no reason to push their way south into the frigid waters surrounding the continent. For centuries, then, no one had a clear picture of what actually lay at the southernmost tip of the world.

Many cultures, however, enjoyed imagining what the southern boundaries of the world might look like. Among the most influential of these peoples were the ancient Greeks and Romans. Unlike many of their contemporaries, these societies knew that the world was round. Moreover, they recognized that a spherical earth would affect the climates of different parts of the globe. That truth had strong implications for the areas closest to the earth's poles. During the first century A.D., Roman geographer Pomponius Mela summed up the conventional wisdom of the day; he wrote a book in which he asserted that the southernmost stretches of the world would be so cold as to be uninhabitable.

In this, of course, Mela was quite right. But the classical image of the world was not always so accurate. Despite the Greeks' reliance on scientific thought, they were subject to many of the same prejudices as any of their neighbors. In particular, Greek culture highly valued the concepts of symmetry and balance. Greek mathematicians looked for symmetry in numbers and shapes, and Greek artists created balance in their pottery and paintings. Greek scientists struggled to find order in the natural world as well.

This idea of balance thus strongly affected the Greek view of the globe. The ancient Greeks knew about Europe, northern Africa, and western Asia, which they saw as connected into a single great continent. To balance this enormous northern landmass, it was necessary to imagine an equally great continent in the south. Some people called this continent the Antipodes, a word meaning the exact opposite (literally, it meant "opposite feet," a reference to the fact that the feet of people in the Southern Hemisphere would point in the opposite direction from those in the northern half of the world). Others referred to it as Terra Incognita, or "unknown land."

Regardless of its name, however, no Greek or Roman scientist disputed that such a continent existed. Greek and Roman maps and geographies all depicted the great Antipodes lying somewhere south of the equator. And since Greek

Like other ancient thinkers, the Greek philosopher Democritus theorized that a massive continent existed in the southernmost latitudes.

and Roman sailors had no firsthand knowledge of the Antarctic—or of any part of the Southern Hemisphere—there was no evidence to contradict this belief. As a result, the idea of a great southern continent took firm root in the minds of classical scientists.

The notion of the Antipodes would persist for generations. Long after Greek and Roman civilizations had vanished, the learned European geographers of the Middle Ages continued to assume the existence of a great southern continent. In time, European explorers would set out on voyages to find the legendary Terra Incognita. In the end, of course, there was no great Antipodes. But as European explorers and geographers searched for the mythical continent, they would eventually discover a different land—cold, forbidding, and unpopulated, but in its own way no less interesting. That land, of course, was Antarctica.

The First Journeys South

The story of Antarctic exploration begins, in a sense, with the theories of the ancient Greeks; but it picks up again with the Europeans of the late 1400s. Before this time, Europeans had showed little interest in the world around them. During the second half of the 1400s, though, that began to change. Led by Spain and Portugal, several western European nations began to send explorers to investigate what lay outside the narrow boundaries of Europe and the coastlines of the Mediterranean Sea.

Technological advances of the fifteenth century resulted in the construction of sturdier, faster ships capable of making long voyages.

Complex forces were behind this new emphasis on exploration. One basic reason for the change, however, was technological. The Europeans were beginning to build sturdier, faster ships that could more easily withstand the stress of long-distance journeys. At the same time, geographers and sailors were starting to develop new navigational tools and techniques. The improvements in ships and navigation both helped make ocean voyages easier than ever before.

A second important reason for the boom in exploration had to do with economics. Over the years, spices, silk, and other valuables had made their way to Europe from eastern Asia. Europeans craved more of these goods, but the distances to Asia were great and the overland journey was long and dangerous. Perhaps, European geographers reasoned, a ship could find a way to make

the trip to the Far East, whether by sailing west—as Christopher Columbus attempted in 1492—or by heading south and then east.

One of the first to try going south was the Portuguese captain Bartolomeu Dias. In 1487 he and his crew became the first to round the Cape of Good Hope at the southern tip of Africa. Dias did not approach the Antarctic; the Cape of Good Hope lies at a latitude of about thirty-four degrees south, which is much closer to the equator than to the South Pole. Still, he had gone farther south than any other European up to that time. Moreover, he had demonstrated that Africa ended a long way from the South Pole. The explorers and geographers of the early Renaissance were delighted by the news. Dias's discovery allowed plenty of room for a great southern continent.

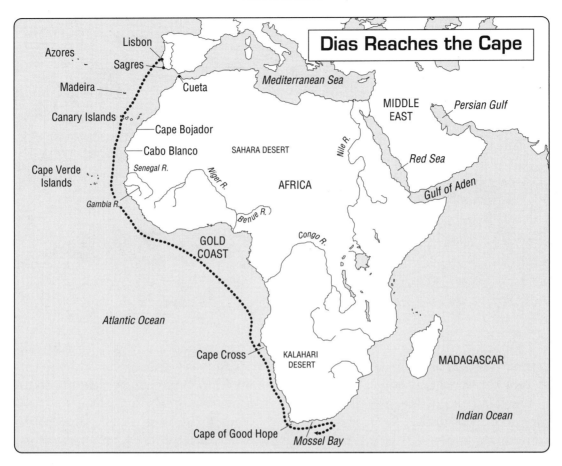

Dias Reaches the Cape

The work of Dias and other explorers proved that Europeans could indeed reach eastern Asia by sailing around the coast of Africa. But their discovery did not put an end to the exploration of the Southern Hemisphere. Now, other countries and adventurers grew curious about what might lie south of the new sea route to Asia.

Ferdinand Magellan and a New Farthest South

Perhaps the next great explorer to head south was Ferdinand Magellan, a Portuguese captain working at the time for the Spanish government. In 1519 Magellan left Europe as the commander of a small group of ships. His intention was to explore the Southern Hemisphere as carefully as possible. In particular, he planned to circumnavigate the globe—that is, to sail all the way around it. Spain, in turn, hoped to claim any new land Magellan might find.

Although Magellan himself did not survive the trip—he died in a battle with natives of the Philippine Islands—the voyage was nevertheless a success. In the end, about eighteen members of his crew managed to complete the circum-navigation. They returned to Spain with important information about the world's southern oceans, much of it previously unknown. In the process of making these discoveries, they had ventured much farther south than Dias or anyone else. And although they had mostly encountered open seas, especially across the southern Pacific and Indian Oceans, they came back convinced that they had found the legendary Terra Incognita.

They had not, of course, but it was an honest mistake. In 1520, Magellan led his small fleet down the eastern coast of South America in search of a route from the Atlantic Ocean into the Pacific. At the fiftieth parallel—the farthest south any European had yet dared to penetrate—the travelers came upon a waterway that led toward the South American interior. Hoping that it was actually a strait, or narrow passage between two larger bodies of water, Magellan decided to follow it. His hopes proved correct. Today, in his honor, this 360-mile passage is called the Strait of Magellan.

The northern boundary of the strait, of course, was the South American mainland. What lay to the south, however, was a mystery. The explorers named this unknown land Tierra del Fuego. Today, we know that Tierra del Fuego is an island, geologically a part of the South American continent. But

as the strait stretched on, the adventurers gradually concluded that Tierra del Fuego was no island at all. Instead, they argued, it was the northern coastline of the elusive continent.

However, there were some potential problems with this interpretation. For one, nowhere else on Earth are two continents divided by such a long and narrow strait. For another, if it was Terra Incognita, it did not stretch nearly as far

Natives of the Philippine Islands attack Ferdinand Magellan and his men. Magellan's expedition passed a few hundred miles north of Antarctica.

north as the Greeks had anticipated. And for a third, much of the rest of Magellan's voyage had been along southern latitudes, without any crewman catching even a glimpse of the supposed southern continent.

But these drawbacks did not bother Magellan's crew at all. Nor did they create problems for the geographers of Europe. After all, there was still room for a large landmass in the Pacific and Indian oceans; it just did not extend as far north as originally believed. Through bad luck, most observers argued, Magellan's crew had again and again steered just north of the massive continent. The Greeks had written extensively of the Antipodes, and so, many insisted, such a place must indeed exist.

The Voyage of Captain Cook

In the two centuries after Magellan, several voyages penetrated farther into the world's southern oceans. A Dutch expedition proved in 1616 that Tierra del Fuego was actually an island, with the Atlantic and Pacific oceans meeting at its southern tip. Another Dutch expedition reached Tasmania, south of Australia, in 1642, before continuing on to New Zealand. And a French explorer sailed across much of the Atlantic Ocean at about the fifty-seventh parallel, well over halfway to the South Pole from the equator.

None of these voyages found any clear sign of the Antipodes. Australia was both

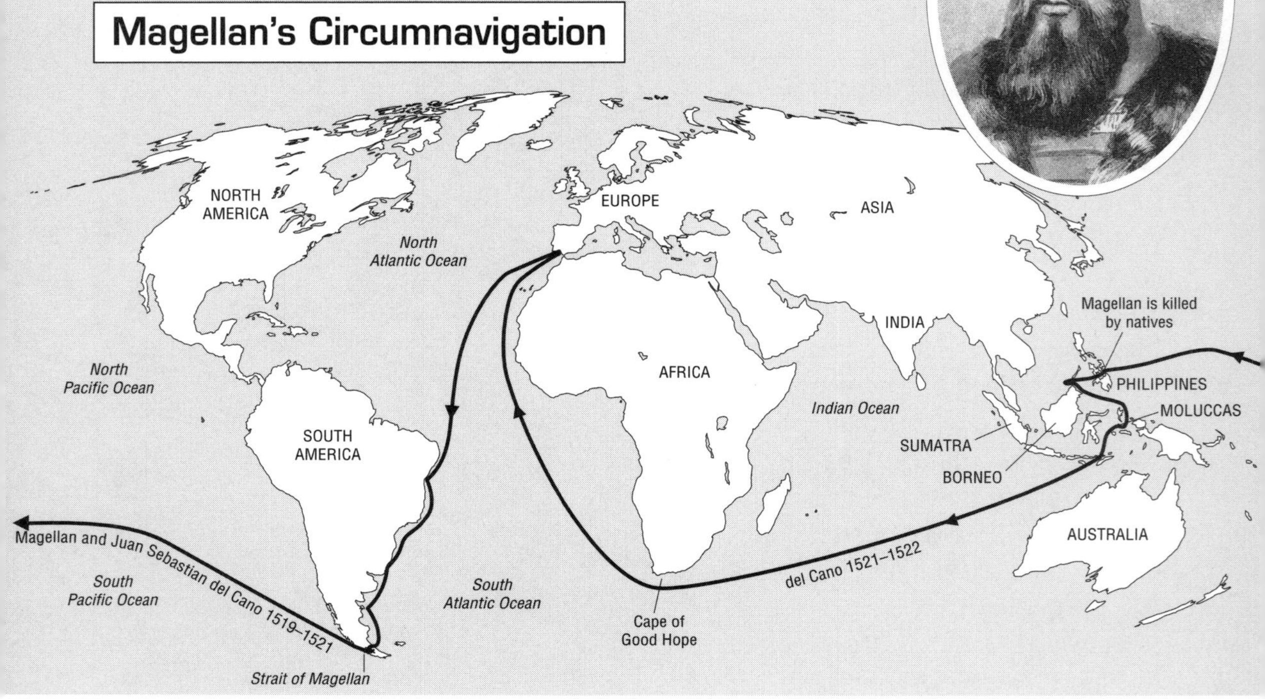

Magellan's Circumnavigation

NORTH AMERICA

EUROPE

ASIA

North Atlantic Ocean

INDIA

Magellan is killed by natives

North Pacific Ocean

AFRICA

PHILIPPINES

MOLUCCAS

Indian Ocean

SUMATRA

BORNEO

SOUTH AMERICA

del Cano 1521–1522

AUSTRALIA

Magellan and Juan Sebastian del Cano 1519–1521

South Pacific Ocean

South Atlantic Ocean

Cape of Good Hope

Strait of Magellan

The Polynesians and Antarctica

If anyone had visited the Antarctic before modern Europeans, the most likely candidates would have been the Polynesian people of the South Pacific Ocean. The Polynesians were expert mariners who traveled across wide expanses of the Pacific in canoes equipped with paddles and sails. Their understanding of navigation was excellent, and they traveled fearlessly from one island chain to the next. Over a period of many centuries, they settled most of the islands from New Zealand to Hawaii.

Moreover, the Polynesians were considerably closer to the Antarctic than any other great seafaring people. The ancient Greeks, the Phoenicians, the Vikings—all were in the Northern Hemisphere, thousands of miles from the southern oceans. But the Polynesians lived primarily in the Southern Hemisphere, and the distance to the Antarctic from some of their islands might have been manageable for a determined crew.

However, there is no evidence that any Polynesians ever voyaged toward Antarctica. Nor is there any good reason why they should have. They would have had little cause to leave temperate and tropical waters, where air temperatures were comfortable and plenty of food was available. Moreover, distances would have made such a journey unlikely, if not absolutely impossible. New Zealand, the southernmost land settled by the Polynesians, extends just south of the forty-fifth parallel, the line that marks the halfway point between the equator and the South Pole. Combined with the lack of any archaeological evidence, the odds are overwhelming that the Polynesians never came near the Antarctic.

too small and too far north to be the great Terra Incognita of Greek legend. Moreover, each journey further limited where a great southern continent could lie. The map of the Southern Hemisphere included ever fewer blank spots. Slowly, a few European thinkers began to question the existence of the Antipodes.

Yet none of these expeditions could completely shake the conviction that there was indeed such a continent. Well into the 1700s, most European world maps showed a massive continent lying just south of the southernmost routes taken by these and other explorers. Some mapmakers decorated this continent with fanciful bays, peninsulas, and nearby islands, none of which existed except in the artists' imaginations.

And other observers went even further. As late as 1765, one British traveler wrote that the Antipodes had a population of at least 50 million scattered across a landmass larger than all Asia. Moreover, he added, the continent was wealthy beyond the comprehension of Europeans. Even "the scraps from this table [that is, the economic leftovers of the continent]," he wrote, "would be sufficient to maintain [all] the power, dominion, and sovereignty of Britain."[1]

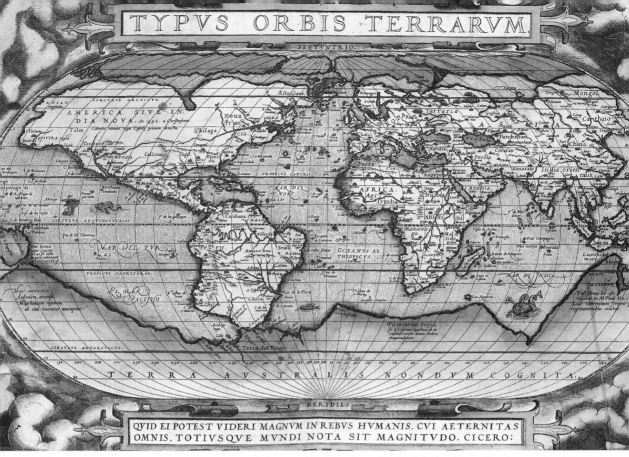

QVID EI POTEST VIDERI MAGNVM IN REBVS HVMANIS, CVI AETERNITAS OMNIS, TOTIVSQVE MVNDI NOTA SIT MAGNITVDO. CICERO:

This detailed sixteenth-century map of the world describes (in Latin) the large landmass in the Southern Hemisphere as a "southern land not yet known."

Still, some people wondered about its existence. Among them were several members of the British government. In 1772 government leaders assigned sea captain James Cook to repeat Magellan's circumnavigation of the globe, only farther south. If a great southern continent did in fact exist, Cook's backers reasoned, then the travelers would surely encounter it as they sailed around the earth at far southern latitudes.

Cook carried out his assignment with care and creativity. Although few previous explorers had ever ventured south of the sixtieth parallel, Cook spent much of his three-year voyage at or below that

latitude. Three times he veered south of the sixty-sixth parallel. His farthest south mark, just past the seventy-first parallel, was considerably south of any distance covered by any previous traveler.

Through the whole trip, though, Cook saw no sign of a large Antipodes. Despite a couple of false alarms—most notably the island of South Georgia in the southern Atlantic Ocean—he encountered no land but small, scattered islands. "I had now made the circuit of the Southern Ocean," wrote Cook when his journey was over, "in such a manner as to leave not the least room for the Possibility of there being a [great] continent."[2] Cook's voyage ended the debate. Astonishingly to some, the Greeks had been wrong: Terra Incognita did not exist.

A Smaller Continent?

Cook had done great work in disproving the idea of a large Terra Incognita. But gradually, Europeans came to realize that he had done much more. Although Cook had not seen Antarctica itself, he had come at one point within fifty or sixty miles of its coastline, and he had certainly become the first explorer to penetrate deep into the Antarctic region. He described this unfamiliar world as one marked by bitter weather—and, most of all, by ice. "Excessive cold, thick snow, islands of ice [that is, icebergs] very thick [plentiful],"[3] wrote a crew member early in the voyage, and similar reports continued throughout the expedition.

Cook had hoped to sail all the way to the South Pole—and would have, he reported later, if not for the ice. As Cook and his crew pressed south, they eventually found their way blocked by pack ice, sheets of ice created when the top layers of the ocean froze. It was pointless for the crew to try to force their way through this barrier. The ice was solid and thick, and extended as far as the men could see. If anything, Cook wrote, the ice "seemed to increase in height as you traced it to the South."[4] Besides, Cook's ships were not strong enough to make the attempt.

The journey was by no means over. Cook sailed along the pack ice, searching for a passage or a crack along which he could venture farther south. Occasionally he found a lead, or open waterway, that offered a way to push deeper into the ice. Sooner or later, however, Cook would find his way blocked by the pack. In the end, he was always forced to make his way back north instead. "I will not

English captain James Cook was one of the earliest explorers to penetrate deep into the icy Antarctic region.

say it was impossible anywhere to get further to the south," wrote Cook about one encounter with a thick ice sheet, "but the attempting it would have been a dangerous and rash [foolish] enterprise [business], and what I believe no man in my situation would have thought of."[5]

In one sense, Cook was relieved to see the pack ice: It gave him an excuse not to travel farther south. With every new line of latitude, the voyage grew more dangerous. Some of the icebergs were several miles long and, as one sailor put it, as tall as a cathedral. Thick fog hung in the air, making it hard for the men to see their way. And the temperature became more and more an issue as the ships proceeded south. "Cold so intense as hardly to be endured,"[6] wrote Cook as they neared the sixty-seventh parallel.

But at the same time, the pack ice was a source of frustration to Cook and his crew. While Cook had demonstrated that there was no room for a massive Terra Incognita, he thought that a smaller landmass might lie farther to the south. "That there may be a continent or large tract of land near the [South] Pole I will not deny," he wrote as he headed home. "On the contrary, I am of the opinion that there is."[7] Somewhere across the sea ice, then, might lie a small continent—nothing to rival Europe and Asia, to be sure, but an interesting discovery in its own right.

This information was exciting, if true. But Cook was of the opinion that no one would ever know for sure. Even if such a continent existed, he believed, it could never be visited. The ice would prove too great a barrier, he argued. "No man will ever venture further [south] than I have done," he wrote. "The lands that lie to the south will never be explored."[8]

Cook had carried out his work well, but he was happy to be rid of the ice-choked seas that had plagued him for parts of three years. He was ready to return home again, and pleased to be done with his southern voyages. Cook could imagine no way in which an expedition might penetrate closer to a supposed continent. But mostly, he could not begin to understand why anyone might even want to try.

The Voyage of Thaddeus Bellingshausen

But Cook was wrong. He had underestimated two human desires: the desire for knowledge and the desire for money. Far from ending exploration of the globe's lowest reaches by disproving the existence of a great southern continent, Cook's discoveries intrigued many who heard about them. During the fifty years following Cook's circumnavigation, in fact, several adventurers explored more and more of the Antarctic—and came gradually closer to the Antarctic Continent itself.

One of the most important of these men was a Russian explorer named Thaddeus Bellingshausen. (Some sources give his first name as Fabian.) Bellingshausen spent the years 1819 to 1821 cruising the Antarctic under orders from Russian em-

James Cook and the Ice Fields

In January 1774 James Cook made this careful observation of an ice field into which his ship had sailed, as quoted in Charles Neider's Antarctica.

An English postage stamp honors Cook's Antarctic voyages aboard the Resolution.

It extended East and West, far beyond the reach of our sight. In the situation we were in, just the southern half of our horizon was illuminated, by the rays of light reflected from the ice, to a considerable height. Ninety-seven ice hills were distinctly seen within the field, besides those on the outside [that is, on the surrounding seas]; many of them very large, and looking like a ridge of mountains, rising one above another till they were all lost in the clouds. The outer, or northern edge of this immense field, was composed of loose or broken ice close packed together; so that it was not possible for any thing to enter it. This was about a mile broad; within which was solid ice in one continued compact body. It was rather low and flat (except the hills), but seemed to increase in height, as you traced it to the South; in which direction it extended beyond our sight.

peror Alexander I. Like his Spanish and Portuguese counterparts of earlier centuries, Alexander was looking for new territory to claim. But he, like Bellingshausen, was also intrigued by the possibility of finding and exploring new lands far to the south. Alexander provided Bellingshausen with two ships, an astronomer, and instructions that included "making investigations, notes and observations of anything which may help in the advancement of science."[9]

In several ways, Bellingshausen's journey was similar to Cook's. Like Cook, he circumnavigated the globe at an extreme southern latitude. Like Cook, Bellingshausen went as far south as he could before being stopped by the pack ice; in the Russian's case, the ice became too thick to traverse at about the seventieth parallel, still slightly north of Cook's record. And although Bellingshausen, like Cook, probably did not actually sight the Antarctic Continent, he certainly did come within about thirty miles of its shores.

Bellingshausen and the Antarctic Continent

Thaddeus Bellingshausen had no reason to believe that he ever sighted an Antarctic continent. His logbooks and journals make no mention of any large landmass, and he never claimed to have seen any land other than the islands he explored and charted. However, some historians, in reconstructing Bellingshausen's travels, think he may have seen the coastline of Antarctica, even though he did not recognize it as such.

Their argument rests largely on Bellingshausen's log entries for February 5 and 6, 1820. On the fifth, the explorer reported seeing what he thought was a large flat-topped iceberg. "Its edge was perpendicular," he wrote, as quoted in Frank Debenham's edited version of *The Voyage of Captain Bellingshausen*, "and formed into little coves." The next day, Bellingshausen mentioned "ice-covered mountains" in the distance. Some observers suggest that he was not actually referring to icebergs at all, but instead was looking at features of Antarctica's shore. Certainly, Bellingshausen's position that day was quite close to the Antarctic Continent, although it is unclear whether he was close enough to the continent to be able to see it.

Today, a few sources credit Bellingshausen with being the first to see mainland Antarctica. Most writers and reference books, however, conclude that his logbook was most likely referring to icebergs, not land, and that Bellingshausen probably could not actually have seen the continent from his position on those two days— or any others during his voyage. The evidence that Bellingshausen saw Antarctica is intriguing, but it is simply too vague to be convincing.

But in other ways, Bellingshausen's travels were quite different from his predecessor's. Bellingshausen focused on exploring the parts of the southern oceans that Cook had not entered. He wrote extensively in his journals about scientific theories and discoveries, particularly those relating to the animals of the region. "It was the size of a hen," wrote Bellingshausen about an unfamiliar bird, "the feathers on the back, wings, and top of the head were brown . . . [the] tail and under part of the body white."[10] His crew collected many examples of the birds of the southern oceans. (Their specimens, unfortunately, did not travel well as the ships headed north, and few survived the return trip.)

In terms of exploration, however, Bellingshausen's most important achievement was in discovering two small islands around the sixty-ninth parallel. "Words cannot describe the delight which appeared on all our faces at the cry of 'Land! Land!'"[11] wrote Bellingshausen; and the excitement remained even after he realized that neither island was actually part of a continent. Still, the islands were more than two hundred miles south of any previously reported land—and they suggested strongly that a larger landmass might well exist across the pack ice.

Sealers and Seals

Although Bellingshausen was the most careful observer of the explorers who visited the Antarctic in the years after Cook's journey, he was not by any means the only man to sail to the world's southernmost latitudes. Indeed, on his voyage he met many other ships, most of them British or American. The captains of these ships, however, were not professional explorers, and they were not interested in the science of the region. Instead, they had come to the Antarctic in search of money.

In his Antarctic travels, James Cook had noted the huge numbers of large mammals in the southern oceans. "There are a greater abundance of whales and seals," reported one of Cook's crewmen, "than I supposed were to be met with in any part of the world."[12] The travelers were particularly amazed to see thousands of seals and sea lions crowding onto the shores of the Antarctic islands.

The seals were not only an impressive sight, though; they represented wealth. Seal hunting was big business. The soft furs of seals were in demand for making coats and hats. Some of the bigger species, moreover, carried blubber, or fat, which could be melted down into oil and sold as fuel. By the early 1800s, British and American seal hunters—or sealers—had killed off much of the Northern Hemisphere's seal population. They were

Huge populations of whales and seals in the Antarctic drew large numbers of hunters to the region during the eighteenth and nineteenth centuries.

ready to look elsewhere, and where they looked was the seal-rich Antarctic.

By the time Bellingshausen arrived in the Antarctic, the sealers were everywhere. At one point, he saw eighteen ships scattered across one small stretch of ocean. There was a good reason for the numbers: The sealers were growing rich off the Antarctic bounty. With few natural enemies, the unsuspecting seals were easy to catch. One sealer told Bellingshausen that his crew alone had killed sixty thousand seals, and later historians have estimated that well over a half million seals were harvested in a single two-year period.

The actions of the sealers, from today's perspective, are impossible to defend. At the same time, though, there is no denying that the sealers were brave seafarers. They sailed across the dangerous Antarctic waters without benefit of detailed charts and maps. While the sealers often did not keep accurate records of their journeys, they nevertheless added immeasurably to human knowledge of the Antarctic. And though their primary intent was to find seals, they did make some important discoveries that had eluded Cook and Bellingshausen.

Finding a Continent

Little by little, in fact, the work of the sealers helped reveal what Cook and Bellingshausen suspected but could not prove: There was indeed a small southern continent. In 1820 sealer Nathaniel Palmer of Connecticut sighted the Antarctic Peninsula not far from the sixty-third parallel. Palmer may not have been the first to see this coastline, and indeed he believed at first that the peninsula was only another of the islands that dotted the ocean at that point. Nevertheless, his logbook remains the earliest clear proof of an Antarctica sighting. In his honor, the Antarctic Peninsula is sometimes known as Palmer Land today.

The following year, another American sealer, John Davis, also made history. As captain of another ship from New England, Davis worried that he was not finding nearly enough seals. Eager to find an untouched island where seals might still be plentiful, Davis steered his craft toward a large and seemingly isolated stretch of land. Lowering a small boat, he sent several men ashore to look for seals. They returned an hour or so later, having found none.

Today, geographers know that this stretch of land was actually another piece of the Antarctic Peninsula. Thus, the sealers who went ashore—history does not record their names—were the first humans ever to set foot on the Antarctic Continent. Davis himself guessed as much. "I think this Southern Land to be a Continent,"[13] he wrote in his log for the day. But still, proof was lacking.

Finally, British sealer James Weddell resolved to determine once and for all whether there really was a southern continent. In 1822 Weddell, already an experienced captain, led two ships on a voyage that would be one part sealing expedition

Although hunters came to the Antarctic primarily to club seals for profit, they also made invaluable contributions to the study of the region's geography.

and one part pure exploration. But to Weddell, the desire to discover land—or, failing that, to sail all the way to the South Pole—won out. Promising a prize to the first crewman to sight land, he steered a course that led far to the south.

Unlike earlier voyagers, Weddell tackled the pack ice directly. Beginning not far from the Antarctic Peninsula, he nosed his ships ahead through places where the ice was thin. By 1823 he had successfully steered past the seventy-fourth parallel, shattering the previous record held by Cook. To Weddell's astonishment, the sea in this part of the Antarctic was completely ice free. As he wrote in his log, resorting to capital letters to convey his shock, "NOT A PAR-TICLE OF ICE OF ANY DESCRIPTION WAS TO BE SEEN." [14]

Unfortunately, Weddell could venture no farther south. The Antarctic summer was running out, and he knew he would have to return to safety or risk being iced in for the winter. Besides, he needed seals to turn a profit on the voyage. He was disappointed not to be able to prove the existence of a continent. (In fact, he had not seen land at all; he had sailed into a sea that would later be named the Weddell Sea after him.) Nevertheless, he had added plenty of information to the map of the Antarctic.

And so had the other men who had ventured into the Antarctic by this time,

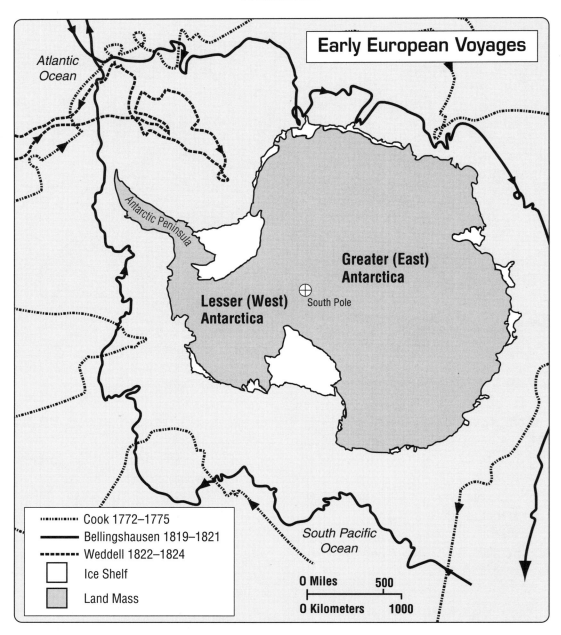

Early European Voyages

Atlantic
Ocean

Antarctic Peninsula

Greater (East)
Antarctica

Lesser (West)
Antarctica

⊕
South Pole

South Pacific
Ocean

•••••••••• Cook 1772–1775
———— Bellingshausen 1819–1821
– – – – Weddell 1822–1824
☐ Ice Shelf
▓ Land Mass

0 Miles 500
0 Kilometers 1000

sealers and professional explorers alike. Between them, they had set the age of Antarctic exploration firmly in motion. Thanks to their work, no one believed any longer in the myth of a great southern continent.

But if the Greek idea of a large Antipodes had been laid to rest, the mystery of what instead might lie at the southern tip of the world remained unresolved. It would stay that way until the next generation of explorers arrived on the scene.

CHAPTER TWO

National Expeditions

The sealers' impact on Antarctica was dramatic but brief. Within a few years these men had managed to destroy most of the local seal population. By 1830 it was no longer possible for a sealer to justify the expense and time of an Antarctic voyage. The sealers left, and the Antarctic waters once again were empty of humans.

Around 1840, however, interest in Antarctica picked up. During this time, a flurry of expeditions embarked from Europe, each of them commanded by men eager to sail through Antarctic waters and investigate places no one had ever seen before. These travelers would add considerable information to the map of the southern part of the globe. Most important of all, they would succeed in settling the question that had troubled explorers since Captain Cook: Was there actually a small Antarctic continent, or was the South Pole surrounded by an icy ocean dotted with tiny islands?

The expeditions of these years had much more in common with the cruises of Bellingshausen and Cook than they did with those of the sealers. Like Bellingshausen and Cook, the leaders of these voyages were not motivated by hope of economic gain. These men were happy to accept that the Antarctic was a barren and frigid land with few resources beyond the now-decimated seal population. None dreamed of getting rich like the most successful of the sealers.

And like Cook and Bellingshausen, these explorers were sponsored, at least in part, by their national governments. Shortly before the 1840s several countries decided to send explorers into the southernmost realms of the world. The government leaders who made these decisions were motivated partly by scientific curiosity and partly by national pride. They hoped that Antarctic explorers might return with important scientific and technical discoveries. At the same time, they expected that a successful expedition would bring their nation considerable prestige.

This time, Russia was not among the nations eager to establish an Antarctic presence. But three other countries were. One was James Cook's England, still among the world's greatest sea powers. Another was France, one of the largest and wealthiest European nations of the period. And the third was the United States, a young nation seeking its place

By the mid–nineteenth century, seal populations in the Antarctic were decimated, and hunting was no longer profitable. The next expeditions to the frigid region were motivated by science.

in world affairs. These three nations would considerably expand the world's understanding of the Antarctic.

"Whatever You Choose to Ask For"

One of these voyages was led by Dumont d'Urville, a French sea captain with a long and successful history of expeditions. During the 1820s, he had made several voyages to the South Pacific, where he had surveyed New Zealand, visited

the coast of western Australia, and visited a number of Polynesian islands. A trained scientist as well as a naval commander, d'Urville brought home specimens of plants and animals from his travels. He also returned with detailed charts and descriptions of the lands he had visited and their peoples.

D'Urville did no exploring in the early 1830s. But in early 1837, by now close to fifty years old, he asked the French government to sponsor him in one more expedition. His plan was to return to the

South Pacific to carry out further studies of Polynesian peoples. To make this expedition seem new and different, d'Urville also announced that he would get to Polynesia by a new route. Instead of sailing east around Africa and Australia to reach the Pacific, d'Urville told government officials that he would head west instead, through the Strait of Magellan.

To d'Urville's delight, the French approved his request. They gave him everything he asked for, and more: two ships rather than one, a crew of nearly two hundred men, and a long list of places to visit in and around the South Pacific. However, French government leaders were eager to establish a presence in the far southern seas, and so they added a twist. Since d'Urville was planning to sail below South America anyway, they reasoned, it would be no trouble for him to make a short detour toward the South Pole.

This part of the assignment dismayed d'Urville. Antarctic exploration did not intrigue him. Worse, d'Urville was no longer a young man, nor was he in good health. He feared that the stress of travel in the far south would be too much for him. Still, his government had spoken, and d'Urville could not refuse. He resolved to do the best he could—and to keep in mind that he would soon be free to continue to the South Pacific.

His decision was helped, moreover, by financial incentives. The French king promised to pay extra bonuses to d'Urville's men if they could make progress into the Antarctic seas. The far-

ther south they traveled, the greater their reward. As for d'Urville, his potential payoff far exceeded mere cash. Should the expedition manage to reach the South Pole, the king promised, he would give d'Urville "whatever you choose to ask for."[15]

A Sea of Ice

D'Urville began his voyage by trying to duplicate James Weddell's route south toward the seventy-fourth parallel. That

French captain Dumont d'Urville led one of the first government-sponsored expeditions to the Antarctic.

decision made sense. Weddell, after all, had found ice-free water at that high latitude, but had been forced to turn back by the approach of fall and by his need to catch more seals. D'Urville, in contrast, had no financial reason to turn around, and he was starting earlier in the Antarctic summer. With luck, he reasoned, he would be able to duplicate Weddell's course—and sail farther than the Englishman.

Unfortunately, d'Urville soon saw firsthand what earlier travelers had only suspected: The amount of ice in Antarctic waters varies considerably from year to year. Weddell had made his trip during an unusually mild year. Relatively little sea ice had formed that winter, and much of what had was melted by late summer. D'Urville, however, was not so lucky. In January 1838, only a few days' journey south of Tierra del Fuego, the ships were stopped by thick ice. D'Urville retreated north and waited a week or two in hopes that warmer weather would melt the ice. Then he tried a new route south.

At first, this route looked promising. The ships slipped gently between icebergs and followed leads, or open paths, among fields of floating ice. D'Urville was pleased. But he had underestimated the Antarctic. After pushing his way into the ice for several days, the weather abruptly turned cold. One February evening, the water around the ships began to freeze. By early the next morning the pathway behind them had frozen solid, and the ships were in danger of being crushed by the steadily advancing ice.

To survive, the crew had to act quickly. "Men climbed down onto the ice to tie ropes to the [ice] floes," d'Urville recalled later. "Those who remained on board hauled on [the ropes] to move painfully forward, while others tried to push the ice aside with picks, pincers and pickaxes."[16] Little by little, the crew picked their way back toward the north, creating a new channel in the tracks of the old one. After five days of backbreaking labor, the men succeeded in escaping the crushing power of the ice. This incident was one of the first instances of Antarctic ships being caught in the pack ice. It would not be the last.

"We Took Possession"

No one would have blamed d'Urville if he had given up exploring the Antarctic then and there. To his credit, though, he spent several more weeks in the area south of Tierra del Fuego, mapping and making observations; and he discovered several unknown islands near the Antarctic Peninsula before finally sailing for the South Pacific. And even more surprisingly, d'Urville was still not totally finished with the Antarctic. In January 1840, while heading home, he made a sudden and unexpected detour. Turning south from the Tasmanian coastline, he headed once again for the pack ice.

D'Urville's motivations are unclear. Perhaps he was feeling guilty over not having gone farther in 1838. Perhaps he was hoping to collect on his promised reward from the French king. Whatever his

Early on in d'Urville's expedition, pack ice trapped his ships and threatened to crush them. His crew had to force a path through the ice using pickaxes.

reasons, he found the seas to the south clear and unfrozen. And this time, the travelers were rewarded. On January 19 a large mass loomed up before them. The men on board the ships knew at once that this was no iceberg. Instead, it was land.

None of the men could be sure whether it was one of the largest islands yet seen in that part of the world, or whether it might be the long-suspected Antarctic Continent. But either way, the men were delighted. "Joy reigned on board," d'Urville wrote in his diary. "The success

of our enterprise was assured."[17] Unable to find a safe way to scale the cliffs in front of them, the explorers did the next best thing. Making their way to a small island just offshore, the ships' officers planted a French flag and drank a toast. Then, as d'Urville put it afterward, "We took possession in the name of France."[18]

The ceremony over, d'Urville and the others retreated to their ships. "We saluted our discovery with a general hurrah," recalled one member of the expedition. "The echoes of these silent regions, for the first time disturbed by human voices, repeated our cries and then returned to their habitual silence."[19] Then, turning north once more, the men headed for home.

The travelers had not found the South Pole, of course, and neither had they ventured much beyond the sixty-eighth parallel. Nor could they be certain that they had found a continent on that January day. Still, the expedition had been a clear success. In appreciation for their efforts, the government divided fifteen thousand gold francs among the officers and crew. D'Urville was awarded some of his nation's highest honors. And perhaps most important, the men of the expedition had once again added to the world's knowledge of the Antarctic.

More Evidence

D'Urville's work would shortly be surpassed, however. In 1838, the year after the Frenchman began his voyage, an American expedition under the command of Charles Wilkes set out for the Antarctic. American officials hoped that Wilkes would learn more about the science and geography of the area. But Wilkes's voyage was also part of a larger plan, one designed to increase American presence in the rest of the world. Indeed, while Wilkes was heading south, other American explorers were investigating the coast of Brazil, the waters of New Zealand, and many other little-known parts of the globe.

Of all these expeditions, though, Wilkes's is the one best remembered today. Yet he almost did not have the chance to make history. A naval officer with a reputation for strictness, Wilkes was actually the American government's fifth choice to lead the expedition. But when each of the previous four men turned down the opportunity, Wilkes was next in line. Although some questioned his ability to command six ships and four hundred crewmen, Wilkes himself had no doubts. Intelligent, ambitious, and brave, he jumped at the chance to lead.

Wilkes's first destination was Tierra del Fuego. He arrived there in late 1838 and began preparing to move farther south when the Antarctic summer arrived in January 1839. Unfortunately, conditions were against him. Thick fog south of the island limited his ability to proceed south. And when the fog lifted, the ice proved thick and impenetrable. Wilkes waited several weeks, but conditions did not improve. Frustrated, Wilkes gave up for the year. Heading back to temperate latitudes, he cruised slowly across the southern Pacific toward Australia, making observations all the way.

Still, to Wilkes, exploring the South Pacific was only a consolation prize. Unlike d'Urville, Wilkes's real interest was the Antarctic, and he eagerly awaited the arrival of the next Antarctic summer. On January 1, 1840, Wilkes left western Australia and led his fleet south once more. By remarkable coincidence, this was the day before d'Urville began heading south from nearby Tasmania. But the connection was random chance; the two explorers had never met and were unaware of one another's plans.

At first Wilkes found the traveling fairly smooth. But on January 11, near the sixty-seventh parallel, the explorers ran into what Wilkes described as "a compact barrier of ice [which] consisted of [ice] masses closely packed, and of every variety of shape and size."[20] Further progress was impossible.

A New Continent

Wilkes was bitterly disappointed to find his way blocked. But having lost one summer to the ice, he was not about to lose another. Moreover, Wilkes was noticing an increasing number of penguins and seals in the ocean around him. While Wilkes knew that these animals could live for long periods of time on floating chunks of ice, he believed that they would not venture too far from land. At the same time, Wilkes saw that the seas were gradually developing a greenish tinge, which he took to be evidence of shallower water ahead. Believing for both these reasons that land might be somewhere nearby, he commanded his fleet to turn west and search for an opening that might lead farther to the south.

The ships moved along slowly, examining the wildlife, the ice, and the waters as they went. On January 16, Wilkes's patience was rewarded. That morning, lookouts on three of his ships sighted a large and distant object jutting out above the ice to the southwest. The object, they agreed, was not an iceberg. It did not reflect light in the same way as the barrier's ice mountains. In addition, it was rounder than the more angular icebergs. The lookouts suspected that they were seeing land—specifically, the peak of a mountain. "I am thoroughly of the opinion that it is an island surrounded by immense fields of ice,"[21] wrote one man.

Although the sighting of land was unconfirmed, Wilkes and his men were intrigued by the discovery. Over the next three days, they continued heading toward the great object. On the morning of the nineteenth, there could no longer be any doubt: The lookouts had seen a mountain, and a large one at that. "[It] had the

American captain Charles Wilkes explored more than fifteen hundred miles of Antarctica's coastline in 1840.

appearance of being three thousand feet in height," wrote Wilkes afterward, "looking gray and dark, and divided into two distinct ridges or elevations throughout its entire extent, the whole being covered with snow." [22]

The ice prevented the men from getting any closer to their discovery. Hoping that they had found something larger than a mere island, though, Wilkes now ordered his vessels to follow the coastline as far as possible to the west. Over the next few weeks, his ships sailed steadily along the sixty-seventh parallel. In some places, ice or poor weather prevented the travelers from seeing land to their south. But in many other places, it was possible to make out mountains, headlands, and rocky coastlines of what was undeniably a great landmass.

In the end, Wilkes sailed along nearly fifteen hundred miles of Antarctic shorelines before being stopped by a massive north-south ice barrier. Turning north, he returned to Australia just as the southern summer was drawing to an end.

The Aftermath of Wilkes's Voyage

Wilkes's voyage would be controversial. Later explorers would prove that some of Wilkes's observations were simply wrong. Here and there, Wilkes claimed to have seen land where none actually existed. This was not entirely his fault. The Antarctic is known today for so-called polar mirages, in which the reflection of the sun low on the horizon can make distant objects seem much closer than they actually are. Like other early explorers, Wilkes knew little of this phenomenon. Still, his errors called much of his account into question.

Nor did Wilkes handle himself well in other ways. Upon returning to Australia, for instance, Wilkes claimed January 19 as his expedition's first sighting of an Antarctic continent. But when he realized that d'Urville had spotted the Antarctic coast on precisely the same day, Wilkes changed the date of his initial sighting. His *real* discovery, he argued, had been on the sixteenth, the day his lookouts made their tentative sightings of land. The statement was reasonable enough, but the swift change made him look grasping and selfish.

For a time, Wilkes's problems threatened to overshadow his achievements. These controversies, combined with allegations that he had mistreated his crew, damaged his career and pushed his discoveries into the background. Nevertheless, Wilkes's expedition had been remarkably successful. He had not only sighted Antarctica, but his long cruise along its coast had demonstrated that it truly was a continent.

An English Prize

Even as Wilkes was traveling Antarctica's shores, a third nation had mounted another important expedition to visit the vast Antarctic. This was England. A small nation with a long seafaring tradition, England was justly proud of its history

This fanciful illustration depicts Wilkes and his men on the Antarctic mainland. Although the expedition never actually made land, Wilkes's long voyage along Antarctica's coast proved the landmass to be a continent.

of exploration and especially of its voyages to the polar regions. The British had led the way in exploring the North American Arctic and believed they had done the same with the Antarctic. James Cook had been English, after all, and so had many of the sealers who had explored the islands of the northern Antarctic.

By 1839 England was ready to outfit another voyage of discovery. The commander of this expedition was to be James Clark Ross. A veteran Arctic explorer, Ross had spent all or part of seventeen summers in the far northern latitudes. More remarkably, he had spent eight winters in the bitterly cold Arctic night. As a result, Ross was at home with polar conditions in a way that no previous Antarctic explorer had been.

Government officials equipped the voyage well, too. They provided Ross with a three-year supply of food, including almost eleven thousand pounds of carrots, and a crew of 128. They also gave him two state-of-the-art ships, the *Erebus* and the *Terror*. These vessels were sturdy sailing ships, reinforced by metal and made stronger with the addition of

John Biscoe and Enderby Land

Charles Wilkes was an extremely competitive man. He was not content to be remembered simply for being the first explorer to offer clear evidence that Antarctica was a continent. He wanted, in addition, to own the honor of being the first man to

This abandoned research facility on Antarctica's Deception Island was built to honor John Biscoe, the English explorer who first sighted mainland Antarctica.

see the Antarctic mainland—the continent below the Antarctic Peninsula. To this end, Wilkes pushed his own claim forward over that of the Frenchman Dumont d'Urville. But in fact, neither Wilkes nor d'Urville was the first to see mainland Antarctica. A little-known English sea captain named John Biscoe had sighted it almost ten years before the voyages of either Wilkes or d'Urville began.

In 1830 an English company known as Enderby Brothers hired Biscoe to head up a commercial voyage to the far southern latitudes. Since Enderby Brothers was in the sealing and whaling business, it routinely sent ships on long journeys. But the firm had a long history of interest in exploration as well. The company's founder had always assigned his crews to make geographical observations wherever they traveled, and his grandsons— now owners of the business—did the same. Thus, it was no surprise that Biscoe was told to explore as well as to look for seals.

Indeed, Biscoe did make an interesting discovery. In 1831, as he sailed through the extreme southern part of the Indian Ocean, he and his men caught a glimpse of mountaintops off in the distance. Over the next few weeks, Biscoe made several attempts to reach the mountains by sea, but the ice blocked him each time. Undaunted, Biscoe named the land Enderby Land in honor of his employers and sailed on. Later, he would argue that the land he had seen, as quoted in Alan Gurney's *Below the Convergence,* "forms the headlands of a Southern Continent."

Despite circumnavigating Antarctica by the end of his journey, Biscoe never again saw any other part of the continent's shoreline. And of course, Biscoe could not be sure of what he had seen. Still, his discovery of Enderby Land remains the first confirmed sighting of Antarctica south of the Antarctic Peninsula.

extra beams. Though a far cry from modern icebreakers—heavy, powerful ships built to batter their way through frozen lakes and rivers—the *Erebus* and the *Terror* were designed to maneuver well within the frozen seas. No Antarctic ships before them had been nearly so powerful.

Ross's first intention had been to explore to the south of Tasmania. But when he arrived at Hobart, the island's capital, he learned that d'Urville and Wilkes had gotten there first. Ross was furious. Earlier, he had publicized his intention to explore that part of the southern ocean, and in his eyes this announcement amounted to a claim on everything south of Australia. Ross quickly accused both his fellow adventurers of poor sportsmanship. In his opinion, they were infringing on territory that should rightfully have been Ross's own.

In a huff, Ross decided not to carry out his original plans after all, but to go elsewhere instead. England, he remarked, should never simply "follow in the footsteps of any other nation."[23] Instead, Ross plotted a new course that would take him to unexplored areas south of New Zealand.

"Grandeur and Magnificence"

As the English government had hoped, Ross embraced the challenges of Antarctic exploration. He sailed south to the pack ice, arriving at its boundaries on January 3, 1841. The barrier that Wilkes had

Captained by James Clark Ross, the Erebus *and* Terror *were designed to safely maneuver through the dense pack ice and choppy waters of the Antarctic.*

described blocked their path, too, but beyond the icy obstacle the men could see patches of open water. Ross never hesitated. He ordered his ships to ram the barrier with as much speed as they could muster—and then to do it again and again, until finally they broke through the ice and the two ships were able to sail into the open water ahead.

Ross and his men made their way steadily south. They passed the latitude at which d'Urville and Wilkes had found land, and still they headed south with no continent in sight. At last, on January 11, the travelers saw a high mountain off to their west. They had sighted Antarctica, too, and at a point farther south of any earlier explorer. Here the coastline ran north and south, and Ross ordered the ships to head farther into the unknown.

By all earlier accounts except Weddell's, travel at these latitudes should have been miserable: cold, icy, and dangerous. But that was not at all the experience of Ross's men. Remarkably, though the men were now south of the seventy-second parallel, the ocean remained unfrozen. The weather was good, too: Ross noted with surprise the number of clear, sunny days they experienced as they headed down Antarctica's shores. Though temperatures remained low, one man wrote that the weather nevertheless reminded him of "the finest May day in England."[24]

And best of all, the sights were astonishing. Earlier explorers may have seen Antarctica as a frozen wasteland, but to Ross and his crew, it was nothing of the sort. Towering mountains, thousands of feet tall, jutted up into the sky; majestic icebergs floated slowly on the surface of the sea. "We gazed with feelings of indescribable delight upon a scene of grandeur and magnificence far beyond anything we had before seen or could have conceived,"[25] Ross wrote.

Volcanoes and Ice Shelves

By January 23 the expedition had gone farther south than Cook, Weddell, or anyone in history. And still they continued to cruise. On January 28, near the seventy-seventh parallel, the travelers sighted two volcanoes, smoke and flames streaming from the tip of the taller of the two. "The discovery of an active volcano in so high a southern latitude," wrote Ross, "[is] a circumstance of high geological importance and interest."[26] But not all of his men immediately thought of science. "It is a sight far exceeding anything I could imagine," wrote one officer. "There is a certain awe that steals over us all in considering our own total insignificance and helplessness."[27]

The journey south, however, was nearly done. Ahead of them, the men could see an enormous floating barrier of ice, this one far too high for Ross's ships to penetrate. As they neared it, they saw just how big it was: a thousand feet thick or more, with the top two hundred feet or so protruding above the water. One of Ross's men described it as "the most rare and magnificent sight that ever the human eye witnessed since the world was created."[28]

Antarctic Weather and James Clark Ross

James Clark Ross was deeply intrigued by Antarctic weather, especially as contrasted with the climates he had found in the Arctic. His meteorological observations were frequent and keen. He was particularly struck by the deep cold of even the Antarctic summer, and he had difficulty imagining what conditions might be like in the wintertime.

In February 1841, toward the end of the polar summer, he explored a bay formed by an enormous wall of ice. To Ross, the sight was reminiscent of "an immense plain of frosted silver," as quoted in Charles Neider's book *Antarctica*. Detailing his interest in the area's climate, he went on to add:

James Clark Ross was greatly intrigued by the Antarctic's inhospitable climate.

> Gigantic icicles depended [that is, hung] from every projecting point of [the wall's] perpendicular cliffs, proving that it sometimes thaws, which otherwise we could not have believed; for at a season of the year equivalent to August in England we had the thermometer at 12° [Fahrenheit], and at noon not rising above 14°; this severity of temperature is remarkable also when compared with our former experience in the northern seas, where from every iceberg you meet with, streams of water [from melting ice] are constantly pouring off during the summer.

The Antarctic, Ross concluded, was clearly colder than the Arctic, and later research has proved him correct.

It was beautiful, no doubt; but it also blocked any further progress.

Holding out hope that there might yet be an opening in the barrier, Ross turned and followed the gigantic ice shelf toward the east, away from the continent. But after a 250-mile voyage that lasted two weeks, he was forced to admit defeat. All along its length, the barrier was smooth, hard, and unbroken. Besides, the summer was beginning to come to a close. Despite his supplies and his Arctic experience, Ross had no intention of spending a winter in the Antarctic. Turning north, he sailed for Australia.

The following summer, Ross returned to explore some of the same regions again. He added substantially to the map of Antarctica. Today, in fact, many of his discoveries bear his name: the thousand-foot-high

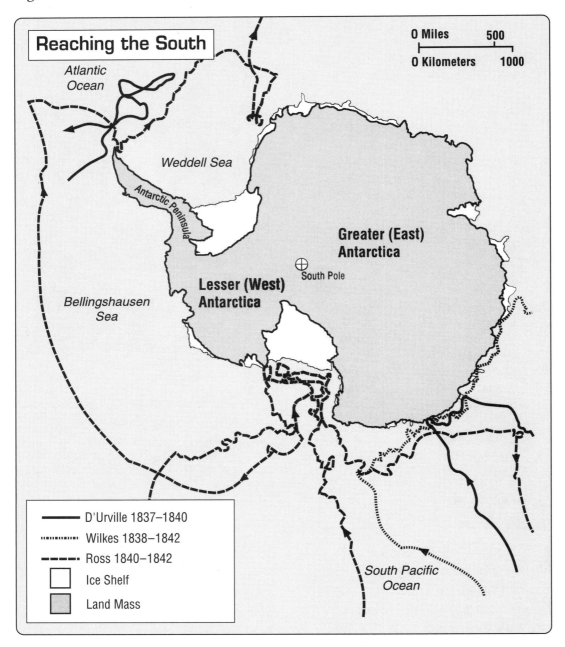

Reaching the South

O Miles 500
O Kilometers 1000

Atlantic Ocean

Weddell Sea

Antarctic Peninsula

Greater (East) Antarctica

⊕ South Pole

Lesser (West) Antarctica

Bellingshausen Sea

—————— D'Urville 1837–1840
·············· Wilkes 1838–1842
– – – – – Ross 1840–1842
☐ Ice Shelf
▨ Land Mass

South Pacific Ocean

Place-Names

The earliest explorers to see Antarctic physical features had the opportunity to name them. The more they found, the more they got to name. Among the most prolific of

The Adelie penguin was named by Dumont d'Urville in honor of his wife.

name givers was James Clark Ross; in the memorable words of historian Fergus Fleming, writing in his book *Barrow's Boys,* Ross began "bestowing names like confetti" soon after spotting the Antarctic coastline. But other explorers, at the time and afterward, joined the fun as well. In most cases, these features still carry the original names today.

Explorers drew names from many different sources. Some were named for friends and relatives. In honor of his wife, for instance, Dumont d'Urville gave the name Adelie Land to the coast he visited, and Ross named an island cape for his fiancée's uncle. Many more were named for politicians, especially those who had spoken up for official sponsorship of expeditions. Features named for important

political leaders include the King Wilhelm II Land, King Haakon VII Sea, and the Queen Maud Mountains.

The names of explorers themselves often appear in Antarctic place-names, too. James Clark Ross is immortalized in the names of a sea, an ice shelf, and an island; the Ross seal, found mainly in the southern oceans, was named for him as well. Ernest Shackleton has a glacier, a mountain range, and an ice shelf named in his honor, Roald Amundsen a sea. While some explorers named features after themselves, these names could also be bestowed on features found by later explorers as well.

A few place-names are simply whimsical. Perhaps the most interesting Antarctic names of all mark features near Pitt's Island, not far from the Antarctic Peninsula. The first visitors to this area gave names such as Buzfuz, Nupkins, and Fizking to the rocks and islets in the region!

ice barrier is now called the Ross Ice Shelf, and the stretch of ocean in which it lies is the Ross Sea. Ross had achieved a new farthest south, and he had seen geological marvels unsuspected by most of those who had gone before. On any list of great Antarctic explorers, Ross ranks high—and justifiably so.

Taken together, Ross, Wilkes, and d'Urville had learned a great deal about Antarctica in a very short amount of time. Between 1837 and 1842, the three explorers, despite representing different nations and regarding one another with some hostility, had essentially proved that Antarctica was a continent, had explored large sections of its coastline, and had brought back valuable information about its natural history. Later explorers would build on this foundation as they undertook their own adventures.

CHAPTER THREE

Living Amid the Ice

The national expeditions led by Ross, Wilkes, and d'Urville did not, at first, heighten interest in further Antarctic exploration. Despite the prospect of an unknown new continent to the south, voyages to the Antarctic practically stopped in the years after Ross completed his expedition. During the fifty years following Ross's adventure, in fact, only two major expeditions traveled anywhere near the area—and neither of them explored the continent south of the Antarctic Peninsula.

This long inactivity was largely because the national expeditions had done their work too well. Before these three voyages, it was possible to imagine almost anything about the Antarctic: that the South Pole was surrounded by an iceless sea, for example, or that the region would prove rich in mineral resources that could easily be extracted from the earth. These prospects were conceivable, if unlikely. But Ross, Wilkes, and d'Urville had demonstrated to everyone's satisfaction that none of these scenarios were realistic. Instead, as one historian put it, they had proved Antarctica to be "an inhospitable lump of ice." [29]

This image of the continent choked off exploration for two reasons. First, there seemed little financial or strategic incentive to investigate such a cold and barren land. No important shipping routes ran through Antarctica, no gold or silver was likely to lurk under the rocks. The seal population had dwindled dramatically; the continent's military value was nonexistent. Through the history of European exploration, the hope of economic or military gain had always been a major reason for exploration. But in the case of Antarctica, those incentives were absent.

And while the continent still beckoned researchers and adventurers eager to reach the South Pole or to study Antarctic science, the reality of forbidding ice shelves and mighty volcanoes appeared to put the region off-limits. Despite their zeal for exploration and their expertise as sailors, neither Ross nor Wilkes had managed to land within sight of the continent. D'Urville, in turn, had gotten no closer than the small island just offshore. The ice, the cold, and the high cliffs along much of Antarctica's coastline had kept them away.

This aerial view of Antarctica's interior shows its rugged mountain terrain and thick ice covering.

Nor was finding a place to land the only problem. Judging from what the national expeditions had observed of Antarctica's coast, it seemed probable that the continent's interior would prove rugged, mountainous, and ice covered. The going would be difficult at best and impossible at worst. The logistics of supplying provisions for a trek south, moreover, struck most observers as overwhelmingly difficult. There seemed little

chance of finding edible plants and animals in the Antarctic interior. Food, fuel, warm clothes—everything would have to travel with the explorers.

Faced with these difficulties, American and European adventurers of the late nineteenth century turned their attention elsewhere. Some headed to the Arctic, others to the highlands of Central Asia or the rain forests of Africa. Without prospects of material gain, and without any easy way to penetrate farther into the continent, there was little point in returning to Antarctica.

Whales and Science

But a half century after James Clark Ross sailed away from Antarctica, the world's view of the Antarctic suddenly changed. One reason was financial. Once, men had headed to the Antarctic to hunt the region's seals. Now, their descendants were back—and looking for whales. Prized largely for their blubber, which could be turned into oil, whales had been hunted for years in the Arctic and in the temperate oceans of the world. But overfishing had seriously reduced these populations, leaving the waters off Antarctica the largest remaining whale habitat. For a few years beginning in the 1890s, the Antarctic whale industry became a moneymaker, just as the seal industry had been seventy years before.

Scientific interest in Antarctica, moreover, was again beginning to rise. Geologists, growing more curious about the forces that created ice ages, thought that the answers to their questions might be found in the Antarctic. Meteorologists and biologists also looked to Antarctica to resolve key debates in their own disciplines. There was no telling what a new generation of researchers and explorers might find. One British scientific panel argued that the continent might hold the answer to the riddle of how life came to be on the earth. "For scientists of many disciplines," points out historian David Yelverton, "such a goal would justify any mission into the unknown."[30]

By 1895 scientific curiosity about Antarctica had reached a peak. An international scientific conference held that year concluded that Antarctica was "the greatest piece of geographical exploration yet to be undertaken."[31] Eager to learn more about the continent, delegates at the conference passed a resolution urging exploration of Antarctica as soon as practicable. They immediately began lobbying governments, scientific organizations, and wealthy individuals for money to send expeditions to the bottom of the world.

The growing excitement about the Antarctic, finally, renewed the interest of adventurers and national governments in the region. Their attention focused primarily on the continent's interior—and on the South Pole, the great prize of Antarctic exploration. True, in the 1840s, and even in the 1860s, entering the icy continent had seemed virtually impossible. But by the 1890s, the task no longer appeared quite so daunting. The late nineteenth century was a time of great scientific innovation, a period in which human achievement seemed to have no barriers. If people were ingenious enough to develop sound recordings, automobiles, and telephones—or so the thinking ran—then surely they could find a way to reach the South Pole.

There were more specific reasons, too, to believe that the Antarctic interior was within reach. Although no south polar exploration had taken place in the fifty years since James Clark Ross's expedition, interest in the Arctic during this period had been considerable. Over the years, Arctic explorers had made great advances in their ability to withstand extreme conditions. They had developed new ways of traveling on snow and ice. They had also found better methods of staying warm. Late-nineteenth-century explorers were sure that these methods could be applied to the Antarctic as well.

The combination of science, money, and glory proved irresistible. Beginning in 1895, ships resumed making trips to the Antarctic oceans. Quite a few of these voyages added little or nothing to the world's knowledge of Antarctica. The crews of these vessels had just one purpose for being in the Antarctic: capturing whales. They had neither the time nor the inclination to seek out new coastlines, find landing places on the continent, or record their routes in great detail.

But other voyages proved much more informative. Some of these were undertaken by scientists, others by adventurers. And a few whalers, like their sealing counterparts of the early nineteenth century, mixed an eye for profit with a keen interest in maps and exploration. In the decade beginning in 1895, these men would pioneer ways of reaching Antarctica's shores—and of spending months or years on the continent itself. The South Pole was still a distant dream, and Antarctica would

never be a hospitable place, but during these years, human ingenuity and will suddenly made the continent a good deal less intimidating.

The First Landing

One of the first of this new generation of voyages was undertaken by a Norwegian whaling vessel appropriately called the *Antarctica*. In 1895, while searching for whales, the *Antarctica* sailed south into the Ross Sea, thus becoming the first ship in that part of the Antarctic since Ross himself. Purely in geographic terms, the voyage was not especially interesting. The ship, under the command of Norwegian captain Leonard Kristensen, limited most of its explorations to areas already visited by Ross. Moreover, it brought back little scientific information.

Still, the *Antarctica*'s voyage expanded the possibilities of south polar exploration. That January, Kristensen steered his ship toward Cape Adare, a point of land in the northern part of the Ross Sea. Years earlier, Ross had spotted and named this cape but had sailed by it without stopping. On January 24, however, Kristensen saw a low spot in the cliffs where he thought a small boat might be able to land. Deciding to give it a try, he and several others made their way through the ice floes and reached the mainland. They stayed for a few hours, then returned to the ship and continued south.

Although Kristensen had not ventured beyond the continent's coastline, he had

Antarctic Clothing

Even in the summer, the cold of Antarctica requires that protective clothing be worn at virtually all times when people are outside. Moreover, the winds common to the Antarctic can make even relatively mild temperatures seem bitterly chilly. It is extremely easy for exposed flesh to freeze.

Over the years, south polar explorers have worn a variety of outfits to protect them from the elements. The first Europeans to venture toward the continent most often wore wool: woolen coats, pants, sweaters, shirts, even underwear. They frequently wore these clothes in layers, because air trapped between the garments provides an extra barrier against the frigid air outside.

Wool generally did a good job of protecting explorers from the elements. However, it had several important drawbacks. For one, it was heavy; a good woolen outfit weighed enough to limit movement considerably. For another, it itched. And for a third, wool kept sweat next to the body rather than letting it escape into the atmosphere. Trapped inside the woolen layers, the sweat moistened clothing and skin alike, making both more prone to cold.

Later explorers experimented with different materials. Some of these were first tested in the Arctic. The Norwegians, in particular, adapted a number of clothing ideas from the native peoples of Canada, Alaska, and extreme northern Europe. Explorers gradually learned, for instance, that fur usually protected against cold better than wool. They made pants a few sizes too large so an extra pair could be pulled on outdoors without an explorer having to remove his boots. And they tried out lightweight, more flexible footgear. By 1900, many of these innovations were slowly becoming accepted, making Antarctic travel easier and safer for a new generation of explorers.

Later Antarctic explorers protected themselves from the extreme cold with heavy animal furs similar to the coat worn by this Eskimo boy.

nevertheless demonstrated that a landing was possible. Today, he and his men are generally accepted to have been the first to set foot on Antarctica south of the Antarctic Peninsula. Moreover, they had done so rather easily. Kristensen's experience emboldened other explorers and scientists. With the landing, the first hurdle toward further exploration had been cleared. Given a foothold on the continent itself, it might someday be possible for adventurers to find a route leading into the vast Antarctic interior.

Kristensen's achievement brought up an important logistical question, however.

Any serious exploration of the continent, whether the coastline or the interior, had to take place during the Antarctic summer, when light was sufficient and the cold was somewhat manageable. Unfortunately, the polar summer was brief. Explorers were largely limited to the months from November to February, though in milder winters they might be able to extend this period on either side by a month or so.

With such a short window of opportunity, expeditions needed to be prepared to set off the moment conditions became favorable. But that required ex-

Icicles hang from the ice covering along the rough coastline and high cliffs of Cape Adare, where Leonard Kristensen's ship first reached the Antarctic mainland.

plorers to spend the previous winter in the Antarctic. Otherwise, adventurers would waste precious early summer days sailing to the continent. Kristensen, for instance, had not landed on Antarctica until the end of January, too late to begin a journey into the interior—and too late to remain on the continent's shorelines for long. On the other hand, Kristensen could not have arrived at Cape Adare much earlier. Until mid-January, the ice surrounding the continent would have been too thick to push through.

Thus, spending a winter in the region was essential for further exploration. The problem was that no one had ever tried to spend a winter in the Antarctic. For that matter, no one had seriously considered making the attempt. Overwintering in the cold and ice of the Arctic had been accomplished previously; James Clark Ross had done it several times. But there were important differences between the two regions. Most notably, the Arctic was full of islands that could serve as landing places for an expedition, while in the Antarctic, islands were few, small, and distant from the continent.

Now that Kristensen and his men had landed on Antarctica itself, though, other explorers wondered if overwintering on the continent might be a possibility. Several, in particular, began to investigate possible methods of doing so.

In 1898 Belgian explorer Adrien de Gerlache's expedition became the first to spend an entire winter in the Antarctic.

The Voyage of de Gerlache

One of the first of these men was a Belgian named Adrien de Gerlache. Compared to Ross, Cook, and other earlier Antarctic explorers, de Gerlache was an amateur. His main qualification for making a voyage was a passionate interest in everything Antarctic. Given little encouragement by his government—in Belgium, complained de Gerlache, "the taste for far-flung enterprises is little developed"[32]—de Gerlache spent months raising money to make the voyage possible. Then he planned an elaborate trip that would take him around half of Antarctica and allow him to explore large sections of the coastline.

That, at least, was the stated goal of the voyage. But de Gerlache probably had another goal in mind, too. Although he never said as much to his crew, there is evidence that he hoped to become the first explorer to spend the winter in Antarctica. Most likely, he had planned to land on the mainland and build wooden huts to ride out the winter. But when he arrived in the southern oceans in late 1897, he discovered that it had been an exceptionally cold winter. Thick ice prevented de Gerlache and his crew from approaching the continent.

De Gerlache was not dismayed. Instead, he changed plans and nosed around the Bellingshausen Sea, just off the Antarctic Peninsula. When the pack ice began to reform in late February 1898, de Gerlache made little effort to head back north. Instead, as the waters froze rapidly around his ship, it soon became stuck fast off the Antarctic Peninsula. Later, crewmen would charge that de Gerlache had deliberately allowed the vessel to be trapped. De Gerlache and his second in command denied the charges, insisting that they had legitimately tried to escape the ice. However, they also added that they were "happy at the failure of our attempt."[33]

Aside from the glory of being the first to winter in the Antarctic, however, the men's situation was potentially desperate. The pressure of the ice threatened to crack open the sides of de Gerlache's ship. The ship carried more than enough food for the winter, but nothing was fresh: There was every chance that the crewmen would contract a potentially fatal disease called scurvy, caused in part by a lack of fresh food. No other ships were nearby; no one knew they were there. The ice was drifting slowly with the current, the ship with it. As summer ended and turned to fall, the sunlight began to disappear. The long and frigid Antarctic night had arrived.

For nearly thirteen months de Gerlache and his crewmen drifted through the Antarctic seas. The experience was miserable. Scurvy did strike the ship; one man died of the disease before the ship's surgeon, Frederick Cook, insisted that the men hunt and eat seals and penguins to stop the sickness. And no one was prepared for the psychological impact of living amid the total darkness, the bitter cold, and the endless sheets of ice. "I can think of nothing more disheartening," wrote Cook, "more destructive to human energy, than this dense, unbroken blackness of the long polar night."[34]

As spring came, the men watched eagerly for a breakup of the ice. Unfortunately, it never came. The weather was simply too cold. In March 1899, afraid that the ice would not melt sufficiently to allow their escape before the next winter arrived, the men began forcing their way through the thick ice to the open seas a few hundred yards away. "We fight our way ahead," wrote crew member Roald Amundsen, "inch by inch, foot by foot, metre by metre."[35] In one place, they actually cut a channel through the pack. Once freed, the ship limped into a South American harbor later that year. It was the end of de Gerlache's career as an Antarctic explorer.

By most standards, de Gerlache's experiment had been anything but a success. Other explorers, however, eagerly studied the Belgian's experience. They saw not failure so much as lack of preparation. For them, the bottom line was that de Gerlache and most of his crew had managed to survive a winter in the Antarctic. Future explorers would try again, equipped this time with better food, a greater awareness of the risks that they faced, and the full awareness and consent of their crews.

The Voyage of Carsten Borchgrevink

It did not take long for another explorer to try his luck overwintering in the Antarctic. In late 1898, while de Gerlache and his crew were still stuck in the ice, a Norwegian explorer named Carsten Borchgrevink led another expedition south toward Antarctica. Borchgrevink, oddly enough, was sponsored in his voyage by an English newspaper publisher. Al-though the Norwegian was already a seasoned explorer, he had failed to interest wealthy backers from his own country in his proposed venture.

Borchgrevink had several goals for his expedition. The centerpiece, however, would be an attempt to spend the winter of 1899 at Cape Adare on the Antarctic mainland. Borchgrevink had been a member of Leonard Kristensen's landing party there a few years before; in fact, he claimed to have been the first out of the boat, and thus the first to set foot on the main part of the continent. His brief experience in the region had convinced him that wintering at the cape was feasible.

Unlike de Gerlache, Borchgrevink had little trouble nearing the Antarctic Continent. He sailed quickly to the cape and set up a camp of wooden huts. Then he and nine crewmen settled down to wait out the polar winter. Keenly aware of history, Borchgrevink was determined to invest his expedition with all the drama he

Members of de Gerlache's expedition were forced to kill and eat seals and penguins to fend off scurvy.

Norwegian explorer Carsten Borchgrevink's expedition spent the winter of 1899 in wooden huts on Antarctica's mainland.

could. "Here we would live or die under conditions which were an unopened book for the world,"[36] he wrote grandly about his attempt to stay all winter on the cape.

Still, those were not mere words. The truth was that Borchgrevink was trying something entirely new—and something quite dangerous. Once the ocean iced over, there would be no escape. Sea travel in and out of Cape Adare would become impossible. Illnesses, accidents, starvation—whatever happened, the men would be completely on their own. They might as well have been on a different planet for all the help any other human could offer them.

Like de Gerlache, Borchgrevink did survive his ordeal in the Antarctic win-

ter. Unfortunately, his experience was not much more successful than de Gerlache's had been. One member of the expedition died during the winter, and the death toll could have been much higher. One man fell into a crevasse, or crack in the ice; an unattended candle almost burned down one of the huts; and three men nearly died of suffocation when a coal stove was accidentally left on. Cold, lonely, and bored, Borchgrevink and his crewmen were delighted to leave the continent in January 1900.

Nevertheless, Borchgrevink's journey was moderately successful. He returned home with valuable scientific data about the Antarctic climate. His expedition had undertaken several further voyages by ship and on foot, and his men had journeyed briefly onto the Ross Ice Shelf and established a new farthest south mark. Most of all, of course, they had gathered important information about staying alive in the bitter Antarctic winter. Borchgrevink's experience, like de Gerlache's, did not dissuade other explorers from exploring the area themselves; if anything, it encouraged them to emulate his example.

Sledges, Science, and the Germans

The experiences of Kristensen, de Gerlache, and Borchgrevink only added to the excitement over Antarctica. By 1900 the scientific community of Europe had secured funding for several national voyages of discovery. One of the most

Antarctic Firsts

Most explorers delight in becoming the first to achieve a particular goal. Throughout history, men—and occasionally women—have competed to be the first to climb a certain mountain, cross a particular desert, or visit a previously unknown island. Antarctic explorers are no different. However, where the Antarctic is concerned, it is often very difficult to determine who was the first to do anything.

Who was the first adventurer to see Antarctica, for instance? The answer depends on the meaning of "seeing" and on how Antarctica is defined. Some argue that it was Thaddeus Bellingshausen, who certainly saw the ice attached to the continent if he did not see the landmass itself. Others accept the account of British naval officer Edward Bransfield, who claimed to have seen the Antarctic Peninsula ten months before Nathaniel Palmer, but whose journal detailing the experience has since been lost. Still others, more cautious, give the honor to Palmer, whose sighting of the peninsula was the first not in dispute. And a few, disregarding the Antarctic Peninsula entirely, give the honor to John Biscoe, the discoverer of Enderby Land.

A similar dispute centers on the question of the first man to set foot on Antarctica. If the Antarctic Peninsula is included, the answer is probably John Davis, the American sealer who spent a few hours on the peninsula without knowing what he had found. Some would argue for Dumont d'Urville, since he reached an island only a few hundred yards offshore. Most sources give the credit to Leonard Kristensen's crew and to three men in particular—crew members Carsten Borchgrevink and Henryk Bull, along with Kristensen himself. But a handful of historians deny even Kristensen's claim; to them, the first people on the Antarctic mainland were Borchgrevink and the nine men who overwintered with him on the continent in 1899.

Because so many expeditions have participated in the exploration of Antarctica, it is difficult to credit any one in particular with the discovery of the continent.

important of these voyages was sponsored by Germany, a newcomer to Antarctic exploration. Like most previous Antarctic expeditions, the German voyage was partly about science and partly about national pride. There was no expectation that the German explorers, led by a geology professor named Erich von Drygalski, would make it into the interior, let alone to the South Pole; but the German government hoped that their men would make valuable discoveries nonetheless.

The German expedition left Europe in 1901. Though the timing of his voyage was open-ended, Drygalski had prepared to spend months, even an entire winter, in the Antarctic. That turned out to be necessary, although not precisely in the way that Drygalski had anticipated. In

Erich von Drygalski's 1902 expedition used dogs to pull sledges into Antarctica's interior.

late February 1902 the German ship became caught in the ice off the Antarctic mainland. By early March, the men aboard were stuck for the season.

The scene was reminiscent of de Gerlache's voyage several years earlier. The Germans, however, were fully prepared for the experience. Drygalski had thought about how to keep a crew healthy, busy, and safe, even through the long night of an Antarctic winter, and he put these ideas into action. During the long winter, the men spent much of their time collecting scientific data. Drygalski used a weather balloon to survey the region and made the first sound recordings of penguin noises. Later, the explorers would publish twenty thick volumes describing their scientific work and experiments.

In this way alone, the German expedition represented a major advance from the voyage of de Gerlache. But Drygalski did more, too. He had brought along sledges, large sleds built to carry supplies and equipment. These sledges, often used in the Arctic, were designed to be pulled across the ice and snow by either men or sled dogs. In theory, at least, they could be used to cover long distances across the polar snow and ice, though only Borchgrevink had tried them out in Antarctica before the arrival of the Germans.

Drygalski wasted little time in sending his men out on sledging trips. Even the ship's precarious position in the middle of the pack ice did not daunt him. By late March, Drygalski wrote, "the situation had stabilized so much that I thought it

The French, the Scots, and the Swedes

The first years of the twentieth century were good ones for national expeditions to Antarctica. In addition to the German expedition led by Erich von Drygalski and a British venture led by British naval captain and explorer Robert Scott, three other nations sponsored voyages to the southern polar regions. One was France, which backed an expedition led by a doctor and avid sailor named Jean Charcot. Charcot had initially been drawn to the Arctic, but soon switched his interest to the much less known Antarctic instead; as he told a friend, as quoted in South-Pole.com. "We have only to get there to achieve something great and fine." Charcot did achieve something fine: He mapped and surveyed stretches of the coast of the Antarctic Peninsula.

Scotland, in turn, outfitted an expedition under the command of naturalist and explorer William Bruce. Bruce was a scientist through and through. English explorer Robert Scott had offered him a post with his own proposed Antarctic expedition, but Bruce had turned it down; not only was Bruce eager to lead his own expedition, but he felt that Scott was insufficiently interested in scientific research. Bruce's voyage was focused primarily on scientific understanding of the Antarctic. During his trip, however, he also visited the Antarctic coastline south of the Atlantic Ocean, marking the only landfall at that time between the peninsula and the lands surveyed by Wilkes and Drygalski.

The most dramatic of these expeditions, however, was one led by Swedish explorer Otto Nordenskjöld. Along with the voyages of Drygalski and Scott, Nordenskjöld's expedition introduced sledging to Antarctica. His expedition would be best remembered, however, for the men's ability to survive even after their only ship was crushed by ice off the Antarctic coast. Their ordeal included a twenty-five-mile trek across the unsteady sea ice, a winter spent on a tiny island with few supplies, and a successful attempt to row a small boat across a stretch of open sea.

was time to start the sledging expeditions."[37] Soon, his men were venturing out onto the frozen seas with sledges and dogs. They were among the first Antarctic explorers to try the sledges on a large scale.

Unfortunately, Drygalski and his men soon found that the going was usually difficult. While it was possible to make good time across the sea ice in favorable weather, traveling on the continent was another matter. In places, the men had to take over from the dogs and shove the heavily laden sledges over ice hills and ridges. Moreover, the sledges had a tendency to fall apart with rough treatment. Nevertheless, Drygalski and his men carried out several successful sledging expeditions, including three to the base of a mountain some fifty miles away. During one of these trips, the men were away from their base for almost two weeks. Ten years earlier, it would have

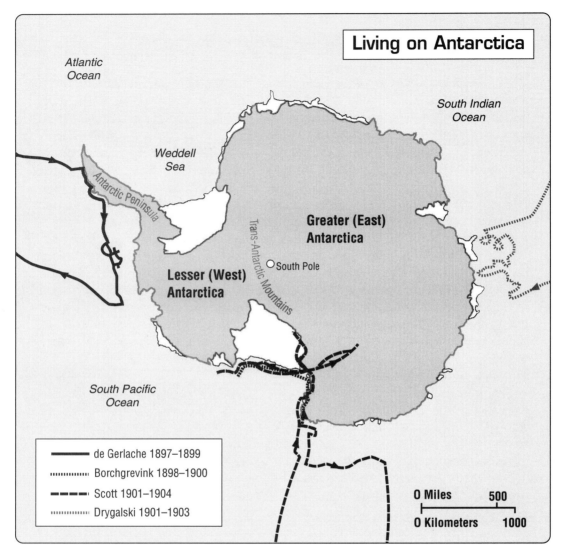

Living on Antarctica

Atlantic
Ocean

South Indian
Ocean

Weddell
Sea

Antarctic Peninsula

Greater (East)
Antarctica

Trans-Antarctic Mountains

○ South Pole

Lesser (West)
Antarctica

South Pacific
Ocean

——— de Gerlache 1897–1899
·········· Borchgrevink 1898–1900
– – – Scott 1901–1904
·········· Drygalski 1901–1903

0 Miles 500
0 Kilometers 1000

been unimaginable for an explorer to travel so far through Antarctica, or to make a journey over such a long period of time. But Drygalski had demonstrated that it could be done.

Among them, the voyages of de Gerlache, Kristensen, Drygalski, and Borchgrevink had dramatically increased the options available to Antarctic explorers. While these men did not explore much new territory, they had much to be proud of. They had reached the Antarctic mainland. They had sledged their way along the frozen coastlines of the landmass. They had wintered both on and off the continent. Their main contribution was not new land, but new ideas—ideas that soon made full-scale exploration of the Antarctic interior not merely a possibility, but a reality.

CHAPTER FOUR

Into the Interior

The first large venture into the Antarctic interior was led by another Englishman, a young naval officer named Robert Scott. Scott's journey was very nearly simultaneous with Drygalski's. He left Europe not long after the Germans sailed for Antarctica and reached McMurdo Sound, where the Ross Ice Shelf meets the continental landmass, a few weeks before Drygalski and his men became trapped in the frozen seas. In early 1902, Scott and his men set up a camp at McMurdo. Once on the continent, they prepared to wait out the winter.

Scott had no previous polar experience, and neither did most of his men. At first, the group struggled to survive at the edge of Antarctica. The men did not understand the realities of the continent: how vicious the blizzards could be, how rapidly exposed flesh could freeze, how many calories a man would burn doing even the simplest outdoor work. One man froze to death soon after they set up camp at McMurdo Sound. "Food, clothing, everything was wrong," Scott would acknowledge later on. "The whole system was bad." [38]

Under duress, the English explorers learned quickly. They found ways of staving off frostbite, and they recognized the necessity of eating more food than they ordinarily needed. The crew spent a rather comfortable winter on board the iced-in ship, which Scott believed would be warmer than the huts in which the men stored their provisions. As had been true aboard Drygalski's ship, Scott devoted the winter months to scientific research. When the men were not occupied with work, however, Scott also knew the importance of keeping his men busy; as one historian put it, "pastimes and debates made the long dark night easier." [39]

While Scott was charged with carrying out scientific investigations, the centerpiece of his expedition was supposed to be a sledge journey south. His government backers, of course, had no way of knowing what Scott would find. It was entirely possible that Scott and his men would find their way blocked by ice ridges, towering cliffs, or horrible weather conditions. On the other hand, it was conceivable that Scott might find a clear path all the way to the South Pole. Whatever the reality, Scott would be the first explorer to venture any significant distance into the continent's interior.

Depots and Dogs

In preparing for his journey south, Scott faced several important decisions. The first was ensuring that his expedition would be well supplied. If he traveled as far into the interior as he hoped, he could not possibly carry all the provisions he would need aboard the sledges. The food and fuel for the return trip would weigh him down, and he would be unable to make forward progress at all.

Instead, Scott used an Arctic method known as depot-laying. The idea behind depot-laying was simple enough. Along their path, the men would place extra fuel, food, and equipment at points known as depots or caches. These items would be carefully sealed in a container, then marked with flags, rock piles, or other indicators. On the way back, the travelers would visit the depots in turn and replenish their supplies. The first depots were to be laid by men who would accompany Scott only a short way into the interior; these men would turn back for the main camp. Later depots would be prepared by Scott and the two men, Edward Wilson and Ernest Shackleton, who would travel the whole distance with him.

If depot-laying was a straightforward process in theory, though, Antarctic conditions made it anything but easy. While depots had been used successfully in the Arctic, no one knew how well the method would translate to the southern polar regions. There was no guarantee that the men would be able to retrace their steps exactly. And Antarctic blizzards might bury caches and markers alike. Still, risky as the process was, it was the only way Scott could hope to achieve any distance south.

Another question was how to pull the sledges. Most polar experts—notably the Norwegians, who had extensive use with sled dogs in their own country—had told Scott to bring dogs to make the sledging easier, much as the German expedition was doing on the other side of the continent. "I find that with dogs it is easier," explained the great Arctic explorer Fridtjof Nansen. "It is . . . cruel to overload a human being with work."[40] In Nansen's view, dogs would save the strength of the men and allow the sledgers to cover more ground more quickly.

However, Scott largely rejected this advice. Perhaps he did not feel comfortable entrusting his life and safety to animals. Certainly, he thought it was brutal to demand that a dog pull a heavy sledge all day long. But mostly, Scott held to a romantic view of polar exploration. Men, he argued, were more noble and admirable if they did the work themselves. "No journey ever made with dogs," he insisted, "can approach the height of that fine conception . . . when a party of men go forth to face hardships, dangers, and difficulties with their own unaided efforts."[41]

Farthest South

Although Scott took only a few dogs with him, he had high hopes for the journey ahead. But in the first week, they managed to travel just fifty miles across the Ross Ice Shelf—a disappointingly short distance. Part of the reason was the stormy weather, which confined the explorers more than once to their tent. The performance of the dogs did not help, either. They were not pulling the way Scott had hoped. Most likely, this was because of his inexperience in dealing with sled dogs. Inconsistent in disciplining them, Scott lacked knowledge of how to motivate them to run faster. Whatever the reasons, though, Scott and his men soon took over most of the heavy hauling.

However, the sledges were fully loaded, and the men had difficulty dragging them south on their own. In rough territory, they had to relay their belongings; that is, they were forced to unload some of their supplies to lighten the load, and make a return trip for the abandoned supplies later on. Perhaps as a result of the extra energy the men used to pull, Scott had underestimated the amount of food they would need. Before long, the three explorers began to ration their remaining food.

Clearly, reaching the South Pole was out of the question. While they might

During most of their 1902 expedition, Robert Scott and his team pulled their own sledges heavily loaded with food and supplies.

Sled Dogs and the English

The sled dogs used in the Antarctic were most commonly huskies. Noted for their strength, stamina, and resistance to cold, huskies were originally native to Siberia and other Arctic and sub-Arctic regions of the world, where they had been used extensively to pull sleds. Many nineteenth-century Europeans who explored polar areas utilized huskies as well. Some explorers arranged their huskies in pairs, like teams of horses. Others preferred to tether them to the sledge individually, in the shape of a fan. Either way, huskies could haul sledge loads much more quickly and efficiently than any human.

Of all the Europeans, though, one group—the English—showed little interest in using dogs. One reason for this was Clements Markham, a retired naval official who served as a sort of godfather to British exploration around 1900. In Markham's day as an explorer, some thirty years earlier, conventional wisdom held that huskies were unreliable. Later evidence contradicted that rather hasty conclusion, but Markham stubbornly stuck to his early beliefs. His influence on later English explorers was enormous, and his prejudice against dogs was widely adopted by young explorers.

The other reason was English society. By the late 1800s, England was among the greatest powers on the globe. It had gotten there, or so its people believed, by virtue of hard work and ingenuity. This attitude was perhaps especially strong in the British navy, the strongest branch of the country's military and the training ground for most English explorers. It was entirely in character for explorers, then, to think that a British naval man could do practically anything he put his mind to do—and, moreover, that he should try. "There was a virtue in doing things the hard way," Roland Huntford wrote in his book *The Last Place on Earth,* summing up the prevalent English attitude of the time. "Dogs interfered with this vision; they made things too easy. That really was their crime."

barely be able to reach the pole itself, Scott knew they did not carry enough food to make the return. With no other means of resupply, the three could go forward only as far as their provisions could carry them home. Still, the travelers persevered. Changing their course slightly to follow the land near the ice shelf, they struggled south toward the eightieth parallel. Beyond this line of latitude lay nothing but blank space on all maps. No one had ever ventured this far south.

On November 25, 1902, the men crossed the parallel. Scott was overjoyed. "It has always been our ambition to get inside that white space," he wrote in his journal, referring to earlier maps of the continent, "and now we are there so the space can no longer be a blank; this compensates for a lot of trouble."[42]

But this achievement was not enough for Scott. The group continued heading south even though all three men were increasingly suffering from their short rations. Each was having dreams about food. Despite the huge effort it took to drag the sledges along, their midday meals were now consisting of one and a half biscuits, a small piece of cold seal meat, and eight lumps of sugar. Worse, Shackleton was showing signs of scurvy. Still, however, Scott did not turn back. Instead, the men pressed steadily on until December 31, when Scott finally called a halt just south of the eighty-second parallel.

As quickly as possible, the men retreated north. It was almost too late. The men were sunburned and nearly starving; their sledges were lighter than ever, but if they did not arrive at the southernmost depot in a timely fashion, they stood a good chance of running out of food and fuel. And Shackleton's condition only continued to deteriorate.

Back North

Fortunately, the travelers reached the depot on January 13, just a few days before their situation would have become dire. "We are not a demonstrative party," Scott reported, "but I think we excused

Scott and his crew share a meal of meager rations. While pressing farther south than any previous expedition, his team nearly exhausted their food supplies.

ourselves for the wild cheer that greeted this [discovery]."[43] Continuing north, the party found another depot, this one containing plenty of extra fuel in addition to luxuries such as chocolate and sardines.

Despite the travelers' delight at finding the depots, the remaining journey back to McMurdo Sound was nevertheless harrowing. The men were physically exhausted, and Scott and Wilson worried especially that Shackleton might not survive. Dragging Shackleton on the sledges when necessary, Wilson and Scott eventually succeeded in bringing him most of the way back to camp. A few miles from the ship, they were met by several other members of the expedition. They were finally safe.

Scott's leadership, to be sure, had been questionable in several areas. His reliance on men rather than dogs to pull the sledges had flown in the face of conventional wisdom, and his handling of the dogs he had brought along left much to be desired. He had badly underestimated the amount of food his men would need. His insistence on continuing south even as conditions deteriorated was an issue, too. Each of these decisions raised legitimate doubts about Scott's judgment and his skills as a commander.

Yet there was no denying his achievements. True, he had failed to reach the South Pole. But he had survived two winters on the Antarctic Continent—one before his journey south and one immediately afterward. He had demonstrated that the depot-laying system could allow explorers to venture deep into the Antarctic interior. He had traveled several hundred miles farther south than anyone else in history, and he had come within five hundred miles of the pole itself. Scott, in short, had established beyond any doubt that Antarctic travel was practicable.

The members of Scott's expedition (from left, Ernest Shackleton, Scott, and Edward Wilson) celebrate Christmas deep in southern Antarctica.

Scott's Other Discoveries

Robert Scott's first Antarctic voyage lasted from 1901 to 1904 and eventually encompassed two full winters at McMurdo Sound. Although this expedition is best remembered for his sledge trip toward the pole, members of the crew made other important journeys of discovery during this time, too. Some found islands to investigate while others explored more distant sections of the ice barrier.

After returning from Antarctica's interior, Robert Scott and his team made additional journeys of discovery along the coast.

Scott went on another journey, too, after returning from his trek into the interior. Late in 1903, he and several companions climbed the Ferrar Glacier, which extended almost nine thousand feet above sea level. This expedition lasted two months and required a journey of over seven hundred miles. The group got lost more than once and suffered badly from cold and exhaustion. Later Scott described it as the most miserable journey of his life.

In spite of the awful conditions, though, Scott and his men succeeded in extending their knowledge of Antarctica through this side trip. They had investigated the glacier and grown to understand more about the continent's ice conditions. They had also demonstrated that the mountains of Antarctica, high as they were, did not present an impassable barrier.

There was every reason to suppose that his methods would eventually lead an explorer to the South Pole.

"Extraordinary Success"

Robert Scott returned to England a national hero. His successes in the Antarctic had captured the public imagination. British government leaders hurried to honor him. Ordinary citizens flocked to see his ship, hear him deliver lectures on his experiences, and buy the book he wrote about his journeys. His fame spread well beyond England, too: An American pamphlet about Antarctic discovery, written shortly after his adventure was complete, referred to Scott's "heroic sledge journey" and called his venture "an expedition of extraordinary success."[44]

But the truth was that Scott was not yet finished with the Antarctic. It was not so much that Scott, like James Clark Ross, had fallen in love with the beauty and wildness of the continent. On the contrary, with few exceptions, he found Antarctica to be a desolate and forbidding place. "Could anything be more terrible than this silent windswept immensity?"[45] Scott wrote in his diary at one point during his expedition; and while these words were written at a low emotional point for him, there is little evidence that Scott especially enjoyed the cold, the ice, and the pristine environment of Antarctica.

But Antarctica did contain a valuable prize—the South Pole. To Scott, in a sense, the South Pole represented unfinished business. He had come far closer to reaching this goal than any expedition leader in the past, and his journey had suggested that a carefully planned and well-executed sledge trip could indeed win the prize. Although for a time Scott seemed content to bask in public adulation, he was nevertheless eager to return to Antarctica and make another attempt on the South Pole.

Fortunately for Scott, the British public was on his side. Locating the South Pole became something of a national obsession within England. All across the country, people pressed Scott to return to Antarctica and finish the work he had begun. The public expected success; certainly it demanded another attempt. "Will the problem of the Antarctic be left where it stands?"[46] the country's most influential newspaper asked in a tone of incredulity. Its subtext was clear: The pole had to be found as soon as possible. It would be unthinkable to stop searching when the goal was so close.

Enter Ernest Shackleton

But in fact the next expedition to explore the Antarctic interior was not made by Scott at all. Instead, it was part of an expedition arranged and led by Ernest Shackleton, the man who had become sick with scurvy on Scott's journey south. After returning to base camp, Shackleton had been evacuated from Antarctica while Scott and the rest of the men remained at McMurdo Sound. Given better food, warmer weather, and an opportunity to rest, Shackleton had recovered.

His reputation, however, had suffered; at least, Shackleton was convinced that it had. By becoming ill, he thought he had failed his fellow explorers, his country, and—most of all—himself. Instead of returning to England triumphantly, Shackleton had come back as an invalid, a man who had crumpled before the challenges of the Antarctic. He feared that the public would remember him not for being a great explorer, but for having ridden on the sledges while his hungry and exhausted companions pulled him to safety.

In early 1907, just as Scott was beginning to plan a second trip to the Antarctic, Shackleton went public with ideas for an expedition of his own. Convincing several wealthy Englishmen to sponsor the voyage, he hastily threw together a crew and an itinerary. Later that year, he left England aboard the ship *Nimrod*. Shackleton's expedition to the Antarctic had begun.

Shackleton Versus Scott

Scott and Shackleton had been friends during Scott's first expedition and had remained close even after the voyage was over. But by the time Shackleton embarked on his own expedition, the relationship between the two men had been stretched to the breaking point. In public, they treated one another with politeness and apparent respect. But in private, each man seethed at the supposed treachery of the other.

The problems had begun during Scott's first expedition, when Shackleton had been unable to march back to base camp and had to be sent home as an invalid. They had grown worse after Scott published a book about his expedition. Shackleton believed that Scott was using him as a scapegoat for having failed to advance farther south (a charge that was probably true) and that Scott had exaggerated the seriousness of his companion's medical problems (which was probably false).

Matters grew worse in 1907, when Shackleton announced his plans to head south. Scott was bitterly angry. "Shackleton owes everything to me," he wrote to a friend, as quoted in Roland Huntford's *The Last Place on Earth*. He was even angrier when he found out that Shackleton intended to use Scott's former McMurdo base, which Scott considered his own property. Shamed by Scott and his friends into changing his plans, Shackleton agreed to look for a base elsewhere. But claiming that he was unable to find anything suitable, he established his headquarters at an island close to Scott's former winter camp—far too close, in any case, for Scott.

The two never entirely repaired their relationship. In the end, the friendship was destroyed by both men's unwillingness to admit wrongdoing, along with their readiness to take offense at real or imagined slights. The problem, for both, was an excess of honor.

A member of Scott's 1902 expedition, Ernest Shackleton later aimed to be the first man to reach the South Pole.

Goals and Methods

Unlike Scott, Shackleton planned to spend just one winter in the Antarctic. But he intended to do considerable exploration both before and after the long polar night. Shackleton had three specific goals, all three of which entailed travel in the interior. One was to climb Mount Erebus, the volcano that James Clark Ross had first sighted over sixty years before. Another was to locate the South Magnetic Pole, the spot toward which all compass needles in the Southern Hemisphere point; experiments indicated that this spot lay within a few hundred miles of the coastline of the Ross Sea.

Shackleton's most important goal, however, was the South Pole. Originally, he had hoped to leave from McMurdo Sound, near the route that he, Wilson, and Scott had pioneered in 1902–1903. In an echo of James Clark Ross back in the early 1840s, however, Scott objected. McMurdo, he said, was his own personal preserve. "Anyone who has had [anything] to do with exploration will regard this region primarily as mine,"[47] he told Shackleton. In the end, Shackleton set up camp several miles from McMurdo—but still closer than Scott would have liked.

To increase speed and efficiency, Shackleton intended to pioneer two new methods of travel during his expedition. One was Siberian ponies. This was an idea originally suggested to him by a participant in Scott's first Antarctic expedition. Strong and accustomed to the snow and ice, the ponies seemed ideal for pulling sledges—especially to a man like Shackleton, whose opinion of sled dogs was no higher than Scott's. While ponies remained untested in the Antarctic, they had proved useful in several sub-Arctic voyages. Accordingly, the *Nimrod* carried a number of ponies on its way south from England.

The addition of ponies was an interesting experiment, but Shackleton's other new idea represented a potentially much more significant innovation. He commissioned an automobile company to build him a motorized sledge—a modified car designed to maneuver in the frozen wastes of Antarctica. Like the ponies, the notion of a motorized sledge had also first occurred to a member of Scott's expedition, in this case engineer Reginald Skelton. "I have an idea that a motor car driven [that is, powered] by petroleum could be constructed to do very good work on [the ice shelf],"[48] Skelton wrote in his journal while in the Antarctic. Later, Skelton discussed his ideas with both Scott and Shackleton.

Between the motorized sledge, the Siberian ponies, and a planned early date of departure from his Antarctic base, Shackleton was convinced that he would succeed in carrying out all three of his expeditions. After a long sea voyage, he arrived at Antarctica in January 1908. Setting up what one observer called "relatively elaborate winter quarters" including "a specially designed hut made of cork,"[49] Shackleton and his men prepared for their adventures.

Mount Erebus and the South Magnetic Pole

The first part of the expedition was wildly successful. That March, soon after their arrival, six of Shackleton's party, including Australian explorer and geologist Douglas Mawson, embarked on their ascent of Mount Erebus. The journey up the volcano was difficult and occasionally treacherous, but the men persevered. Once at the top of the 13,500-foot mountain, the men measured the volcanic crater, took multiple photographs, and gathered rock samples. Once finished, they quite literally slid back down the way they had come. The ice and snow provided an ideal, if hazardous, sledding hill, and the men took full advantage of the opportunity. At one point, the men careened down five thousand feet of the steep slope in about four hours.

The second of Shackleton's proposed expeditions left winter camp in September 1908. This was the journey to the South Magnetic Pole. This part of

Shackleton contracted with an automobile company to build a motorized sledge similar to this one to help his expedition reach the South Pole.

the expedition was led by English scientist Edgeworth David, with Mawson as one of the participants. Shackleton dubbed this expedition the Northern Party to distinguish it from the Southern Party, which would later head south to search for the South Pole itself.

The Northern Party, unfortunately, did not have as smooth a trip as the group that had climbed Mount Erebus earlier in the year. Most of the members of the Northern Party had little previous polar experience, and the long trek across the Antarctic ice proved almost too much for them to handle. Food was one problem: As on Scott's journey south, the men had underestimated how much they would need to eat, and the party very quickly had to go on short rations. Accidents

were another: Both David and Mawson fell into crevasses and had to be rescued by their companions.

But the biggest issue was that the men were forced to pull their sledges by hand. Neither the ponies nor the motorized sledge worked out as Shackleton had hoped. The sea voyage to Antarctica had been terribly hard on the ponies; one died upon arrival and the rest were in poor shape by the time the *Nimrod* arrived. Moreover, the ponies ate no meat. There was no food for them anywhere on Antarctica, so all their food had to be brought in from outside the continent. The grain they required took up a great deal of space, both on the *Nimrod* and especially as the explorers traveled inland. By the time the Northern Party be-

The inexperience of some of Shackleton's men resulted in several accidents. Two of his crew fell into crevasses and had to be rescued like this modern-day explorer.

Because the motorized sledge failed to work as planned, Shackleton's crew was forced to haul their supply sledges themselves during the expedition. Shackleton's men, though, like most English explorers in Antarctica at the time, only traveled on skis sparingly.

gan its journey, few ponies remained. None accompanied the group on its trek to the magnetic pole.

The motorized sledge was not much more effective. It held up long enough to lay two depots on the nearby ice for the Northern Party. Then it stopped working, its engine broken beyond repair. The bitter cold and the unyielding ice surface had proved too much for it. Members of the Northern Party had hoped to have the use of the sledge for many more miles, but that was not to be. Without motorized sledges, ponies, or dogs, they would have to make do with their own hauling power instead.

Despite the expense of energy, the insufficient food, and the frequent mishaps, the men struggled on. On January 15, nearly three months after their journey

had begun, the men finally reached the South Magnetic Pole. They claimed the area for England, gave three cheers, and then immediately began hurrying back toward the base camp. By late February, down almost to their last few bites of food, they met up with the *Nimrod* and were enjoying hot baths and warm bunks.

David and Mawson were justifiably delighted with their success. They had explored a previously unknown section of Antarctica and had survived a dramatic and dangerous journey. "We pioneered a route to the magnetic pole," David observed, "and we hope that the path thus found will prove of use to future observers."[50] However, the trek had taken a severe toll. The twelve-hundred-mile round-trip was difficult enough for novice explorers; it had been made that much more exhausting by the lack of dogs to haul the sledges. With sled dogs, David argued afterward, the group could have made the journey in about half the time.

Shackleton Heads South

About a month after Mawson and David began their trek to the South Magnetic Pole, Shackleton and three of his men began their own journey into the Antarctic interior. At first, the explorers moved slowly. They experienced the same problem with crevasses as the members of the Northern Party, and the perpetually overcast skies made it difficult to identify ice hills, ridges, and other natural features against the monotonous horizon. Picking their way forward was difficult—and dangerous.

Shackleton still held out hope that the surviving ponies would be of use on the trip, but he was quickly disappointed. By the end of November, all but one of the ponies had died, victims of the cold and the exhausting work of sledging. Fortunately for the explorers, the meat from the dead animals added to the group's rapidly shrinking supply of food. The men ate some of the pony meat on the spot and cached the rest for their return trip.

Conditions improved slowly for Shackleton and his party. On November 20, they passed the eighty-second parallel, thereby beating Scott's former farthest south mark. Soon after that, they moved off the Ross Ice Shelf and onto the continent itself. Here they were met with the Beardmore Glacier, a gigantic pile of ice sloping steadily up into the interior. As quickly as they could, the men ascended the slope, hoping that they would have easy access south to the pole once they reached the glacier's top.

Unfortunately, the climb up the glacier was far from smooth. Ridges of ice blocked their way in places; crevasses yawned ahead of them. The men reached an altitude of five thousand feet above sea level, then ten thousand. Frustration reigned as the glacier continued without end and the hoped-for flat surface south remained elusive. "Tomorrow we will throw away everything except the most absolute necessities," Shackleton wrote on Christmas Day. "Every time we reach the top of a ridge we say 'perhaps this is the last,' but it never is the last."[51]

Onto the Polar Plateau

But a few days after Christmas, the men noted a gradual flattening of the ice in front of them. It was soon clear that they were off the glacier; though they were still ascending, the slope was considerably gentler. Shackleton was pleased, if unwilling to rejoice. "If a great snow plain, rising every seven miles in a steep ridge, can be called a plateau," Shackleton wrote in his diary, referring to the flat, easily traveled surface he had hoped to find, "then we are on it at last."[52]

By now, though, they were running out of time. The men struggled onward, but Shackleton knew the truth. After two months on the trail, he and his companions were in poor physical condition, and their food supplies had become seriously low. On January 4, Shackleton told his men that they would soon have to give up their quest. Finally, on January 9, 1909, shortly after a vicious blizzard struck the area, Shackleton reluctantly ordered the group to turn around and head for their base.

It must have been an agonizingly difficult decision. The men had surpassed the eighty-eighth parallel and shattered Scott's previous farthest south mark by 360 miles. They had traversed the entire Ross Ice Shelf, reached the continent, and ascended the length of the Beardmore Glacier. They had come within ninety-seven miles of the South Pole. Yet

After Shackleton's expedition labored to reach the plateau of Beardmore Glacier (pictured), harsh weather and dwindling supplies forced them to return to base camp.

Pictured is Shackleton's base camp on the Ross Ice Shelf. Shackleton's expedition ventured beyond the eighty-eighth parallel before being forced to return to camp.

Shackleton chose to turn around. By this time a seasoned Antarctic explorer, he knew that he and his men would surely die if they went any farther. Later, he would justify his decision to his wife with the words: "I thought you would rather have a live donkey than a dead lion."[53]

Still, Shackleton's journey into the interior ranked among the greatest of all polar explorations. Without dogs, without much help from ponies, and with no clear notion of what they would encounter past the end of the ice shelf, Shackleton and his men had performed admirably. They had charted and explored hundreds of miles of territory along the Beardmore and beyond. Combined with the expedition's successes on Mount Erebus and at the South Magnetic Pole, Shackleton's trek toward the South Pole had added a great deal to the map of Antarctica.

CHAPTER FIVE

The Race to the Pole

With Shackleton having gotten so close, no one doubted that reaching the South Pole was possible. The only remaining questions were who would get there first and when it would happen. It was only a matter of planning a trip that would succeed in getting a group of men all the way to the South Pole—the great prize of Antarctic exploration—and then getting them safely back again.

The field was now open for Scott to finish the work he had begun. Gathering backers of his own from government and private sources, he outfitted a ship, the *Terra Nova,* to carry men and equipment from England to his old base on Mc-Murdo Sound. Like Shackleton, Scott decided to rely not on dogs but on ponies and a motorized sledge of his own design. His natural distrust of sled dogs had been heightened by their poor showing on his own earlier journey toward the Pole. Moreover, Shackleton's ability to get so far south without them convinced Scott that dogs were unnecessary.

Scott's interest in finding the South Pole was apparent to all who knew him. "The main object of the expedition," he announced once, "is to reach the South Pole and secure for The British Empire the honour of this achievement." [54] Nevertheless, Scott made it clear that this voyage was not dedicated simply to reaching that goal. Scott's plans included scientific investigation and other journeys of discovery as well. While reaching the pole was vital to Scott, he was not willing to make it the only purpose of his expedition.

In early 1910 the *Terra Nova* left England. Spirits aboard the ship were high. So far as reaching the South Pole was concerned, Shackleton seemed to be Scott's only other competitor, and Shackleton was not in a position to mount another expedition for some time to come. With a newly designed motor sledge, a herd of ponies, and the unquenchable will of the men themselves, Scott and his crew were certain that they would succeed in finding the pole at last.

But on the *Terra Nova*'s voyage south, the ship pulled into an Atlantic port to replenish supplies. There, Scott received unwelcome news. A telegram was waiting for him, sent by Norwegian explorer Roald Amundsen. The message was brief and to the point. "Am going south," [55] it read.

Robert Scott's ship, the Terra Nova, *reaches Antarctica in 1910. Scott returned to Antarctica in an attempt to complete the journey to the South Pole.*

Roald Amundsen

Roald Amundsen represented stiff competition indeed. He was perhaps the greatest polar explorer of his time—or any other. Most of his expeditions had been confined to the Arctic. In 1905 he had completed a voyage through the Northwest Passage in the Canadian Arctic, becoming the first person to travel the waterways of these far northern lands by boat. He had visited the North Magnetic Pole—discovered originally by James Clark Ross—and proved that this point was not fixed relative to the earth, but rather moved from year to year.

However, Amundsen had some Antarctic experience, too. He had been a valued crew member aboard Adrien de Gerlache's 1898–1899 expedition. Unlike many of the others on that near-disastrous voyage, he had been intrigued by the beauty of the far southern regions of the world. In the romantic words of historian Alan Gurney, he "thought the continent a sleeping beauty awaiting her kiss."[56] At the time, he had vowed to return someday. Now, that time had come.

The reason, simply put, was glory. For years, Amundsen had hoped to be the first person to reach the North Pole. But in 1909, American Robert Peary had apparently beaten him to it. Arriving home after a long expedition to the Canadian Arctic, Peary announced that he had reached the pole. Publicly, Amundsen congratulated Peary and insisted that he would continue with his plans to reach the pole himself. But privately, Amundsen found Peary's news devastating.

Today, there is much debate over the validity of Peary's claims. Many experts have concluded that Peary never reached the pole at all. But at the time, Amundsen saw no reason to challenge the American's assertions. Instead, he devised a bold plan. A seasoned polar explorer, he turned his attention to the Antarctic instead. Reading everything he could find about the continent, Amundsen made up his mind: If he could not be the first to

Rival polar explorers (from left) Ernest Shackleton, Robert Peary, and Roald Amundsen. Peary had been first to the North Pole, and Amundsen raced to be first to the South Pole.

the North Pole, then he would be the first to the South Pole.

However, Amundsen shared his plans with almost no one. A secretive person under any circumstances, he was especially reluctant to divulge his Antarctic intentions. In particular, Amundsen was in no hurry to tip off Scott. If it became known that another explorer was interested in the pole, he feared, the British would quickly increase the funding for Scott's expedition—leaving him little chance to reach the pole before the Englishman. Besides, Amundsen had told his own backers that he was sailing for the North Pole, and he suspected that they might not keep their financial promises to him if he were to sail elsewhere.

As a result, when Amundsen's ship left Norway, only a handful of people knew its actual destination. Even the crew did not learn the truth until the ship reached Madeira in the Atlantic Ocean—the point when Amundsen cabled Scott to give him the news. At first, of course, the men were shocked. But once the men got over their initial surprise, they joined forces behind their commander. Amundsen and his men quickly headed south. Leaving Scott his base at McMurdo Sound, they set up winter quarters of their own at the Bay of Whales farther along the Ross Ice Shelf.

Igloos, Skis, and Dogs

Amundsen and Scott were very different people, and their attitude toward exploration was not at all the same. Most no-

table, perhaps, were the two men's backgrounds. Amundsen was in a sense a professional explorer. He had done very little in his adult life other than make discoveries; his résumé included one adventurous voyage after another. Scott, in contrast, was a gentleman amateur. He had spent the bulk of his career as a naval officer, and by 1910 he had just one significant expedition to his credit.

Another important difference involved the two men's understanding of polar conditions. Amundsen's experience in the far north had given him knowledge that Scott simply did not have. After wintering among natives in the Canadian Arctic, for instance, Amundsen had learned to handle a kayak, build a snow house, and dress in traditional Inuit clothing. None of these skills, in contrast, had been mastered by Scott and his men. "Played at building an igloo—with no success,"[57] one of Scott's men reported in his diary after reaching their winter quarters.

The two men differed as well in their preferred methods of transportation. While Scott did not trust sled dogs, for instance, Amundsen was convinced that reaching the South Pole would be almost impossible without them. Thus, while Scott brought ponies and motorized sledges to his base at McMurdo Sound, Amundsen brought only dogs to his base down the ice barrier. Moreover, Amundsen, like all his men, was an experienced skier, and Amundsen had found that this method was generally preferable to walking through the snow and ice. In contrast, few of Scott's men were comfortable on skis. Thus, they had no choice but to walk.

Amundsen Sets Off

Scott was puzzled and infuriated by Amundsen's telegram. Echoing Ross's complaint about Wilkes and d'Urville, Scott believed that he should have priority of discovery where the South Pole was concerned. However, he knew he had no power to forestall the Norwegians. Scott decided that he would try to ignore Amundsen altogether. "The proper, as well as the wiser, course for us is to proceed exactly as though this had not happened,"[58] he wrote. Reaching his McMurdo base in January 1911, he supervised the unloading of the *Terra Nova* and the setting up of winter quarters. He chose not to advance his schedule to try to reach the pole before his rival.

At the other end of the ice shelf, though, Amundsen was not prepared to ignore Scott. Although Amundsen had carried out important scientific discoveries in the past, this expedition had no scientific plans whatever. Amundsen was in Antarctica solely to be the first to the South Pole. Following his arrival, he immediately set to work laying depots for the next summer's trek south. Before winter came, he and his men had successfully cached food, fuel, and equipment all

American explorer Robert Peary, pictured on the deck of his ship during his 1909 expedition to the North Pole.

along the Ross Ice Shelf—almost halfway to the pole.

In October Amundsen and his men got under way. At first, the travelers made excellent time across the ice. "Dogs as if possessed," wrote one of Amundsen's four companions, "careered off like madmen. Going good and terrain flat and

Eating the Transportation

For Roald Amundsen, sled dogs served two purposes: they were at once transportation and food. Generations of polar explorers had realized that making long sledge voyages was a complicated business. It was important to carry enough food for the journey, especially if—as in the Antarctic interior—there was no chance of getting any more during the trip. Carrying too much food, however, weighed down the sledges and slowed the travelers. The trick was in finding the perfect balance between too much and too little.

The issue was even trickier if dogs were being used. The huskies had to be fed, too, which meant packing extra weight in the form of food for the dogs. (On polar expeditions, the dogs often ate similar foods to what the men brought for themselves.) The heavier the sledge, the more dogs were needed; but the greater number of dogs in turn required more food and therefore a heavier sledge load. Again, it was essential to strike a balance between having too many dogs and not enough.

One solution to this dilemma was to make double use of at least some of the dogs. Early in the journey, when sledges were piled high with supplies, explorers  made sure to bring along plenty of huskies. At a certain point during the trip, though, the sledges would be significantly lighter, and all that pulling power would no longer be necessary. Then, the explorers would kill several of the weaker dogs. They would eat some of the meat themselves, feed some to the surviving dogs, and cache the remaining carcasses if a return trip was planned.

The system was undeniably cruel, and Amundsen, at least, was sorry to pull the trigger. But it worked. The butchering of the dogs provided a new supply of fresh food that did not have to be carried on the sledges. It fed men and the surviving dogs alike. The system helped Amundsen reach the South Pole as easily as he did.

fine."[59] The hauling power of the dogs permitted the men to save more of their energy, too. Because of that, Amundsen and his men needed less food than the members of the earlier expeditions led by Scott and Shackleton. Where the two British explorers had quickly found themselves cutting rations, Amundsen's men continued to eat all they needed.

Amundsen took a different route over the ice shelf from the one that Scott and Shackleton had pioneered. Rather than head for the Beardmore Glacier, he was eager to discover what lay at the other end of the ice. By early November, he had reached the mountains at the edge of the continent. On the side of this mountain range was the previously unknown Axel Heiberg Glacier, not as large as the Beardmore, but still massive enough to present a major obstacle to forward progress.

Amundsen faced a decision. He could take the time to scout the mountains for a relatively easy pass through the slopes, or he could simply plow straight south. Despite the forbidding height of the mountains ahead, he chose the second option. The men immediately began forcing their sledges uphill across the glacier ice and the rocky ledges. The path was dangerous and technically difficult. But after four days of hard work, they had succeeded. Amundsen's men had ascended nearly two miles of elevation, bringing their fully loaded sledges and forty dogs.

"So We Arrived"

The effort had been worth the explorers' while. From this spot at the top of the glacier, Amundsen and his men had a relatively smooth and flat journey ahead of them. To be sure, there were hardships: ridges of snow and ice known as sastrugi; howling winds from the south that prevented the travelers from moving forward; overcast skies that made visibility difficult. "What does [this] crevasse look like?" Amundsen inquired once when one of the sledges nearly fell into one.

"Oh, as usual," one of his men told him. "No bottom."[60]

But nothing on the polar plateau compared to the dangers of the mountains, and the travelers pushed steadily onward. By early December they reached the eighty-eighth parallel, Shackleton's previous record. They were in far better physical condition than Shackleton and his men had been—and it was earlier in the polar summer, too. "We all shook hands, with mutual congratulations," Amundsen wrote later. "We had won our way . . . by holding together, and we would go farther yet—to the end."[61]

The end was not far off. On December 15, 1911, they reached the South Pole. It was evident that no one had been there; they had defeated Scott and his companions. The men put up the Norwegian flag and pitched a tent containing some spare equipment. Both would stand as proof of their achievement. "So we arrived," Amundsen wrote in his diary, "and were able to plant our flag at the geographic South Pole. God be thanked!"[62] The men spent two days exploring and charting the general area. Then they began the return trip to the Bay of Whales, arriving in good health about six weeks later.

Scott's Arrival

Robert Scott's expedition, on the other hand, would prove very different from his rival's. Like Shackleton, Scott found that the ponies he had brought were largely ineffective in the Antarctic climate; like Shackleton, too, Scott did not get the benefit he hoped from his own motorized sledge. Thus, once again, Scott and his men were reduced to hauling sledges by hand as they crossed the Ross Ice Shelf and began the ascent up the Beardmore.

The extra expense of energy, of course, required more food, and once again, rations were in short supply. Worse, the expedition was meeting with unusually stormy weather, and several of the men were showing signs of illness. Hungry, coughing, and cold, the men nevertheless struggled onward.

In early January, Scott and the four companions he had chosen for the final push passed the southern limit of Shackleton's voyage. They were now less than a hundred miles from the pole. Despite the hardships thus far, and despite the fact that they had already eaten some of the food earmarked for the trek home, the men were in reasonably good spirits. As far as they knew, they had traveled farther south than anyone else in history.

But their mood was dashed on January 16. Just a few miles from the pole, Scott and his men encountered dog and sledge tracks. Amundsen had been there first. Deeply discouraged, the travelers marched on another day to the pole. Scott recorded the moment in his diary: "The Pole. Yes, but under very different circumstances from those expected. . . . Great God! This is an awful place and terrible enough for us to have laboured to it without the reward of priority [that is, being first]."[63]

The men headed for home as soon as possible. But the lessened rations and the bitter cold had taken their toll. In order to return successfully to McMurdo, Scott needed absolutely perfect conditions, but that was not what he got. Blizzard after blizzard forced the travelers to stop. The party lost valuable time searching for one depot. When they reached another, they found that much of the fuel, needed for warmth as well as for cooking, had somehow leaked out. Still, the men limped along, hauling sledges that by now carried very little food—but which did include thirty pounds of rock samples from the South Pole.

Unfortunately, the conditions were too much. One man died in February, another in early March. The three survivors, including Scott, struggled on, but their situation was growing more desperate by the hour. In late March they ran into yet another blizzard just a few miles from a depot. This delay cost them the remainder of their cooking fuel—and the last of their food. Robert Scott's last diary entry, dated March 29, 1912, told the rest of the story:

Outside the door of our tent it remains a scene of whirling wind. I do not think we can hope for any better things now. We shall stick it out to the end, but we are getting weaker, of course, and the end cannot be far. It seems a pity, but I do not think I can write more. For God's sake look after our people.[64]

There were, indeed, no "better things" ahead for Scott and his companions.

Circling the Pole

Amundsen had no way to tell precisely whether he was at the South Pole. The instruments at his disposal were not accurate enough to measure his latitude and longitude within more than a few miles. Once he arrived at what he thought was the pole, he was not yet through.

Amundsen assigned his men to split up. Singly or in pairs, they would all go another twelve and a half miles in each of three directions: to the left, to the right, and forward. This process was called "boxing" the area, though "circling" might have been a better name. After the men had carried this out, they had reached three points on the outside of an imaginary circle twenty-five miles across, with its center at the spot where they believed the South Pole to be. Including their route to the area, they had now reached four points, each twelve and a half miles from the supposed South Pole. By convention, if the pole was actually anywhere inside this circle, Amundsen's men could claim to have been there.

In fact, Amundsen's measurements were a good deal more accurate than that. Later investigation revealed that his chosen spot was just over a mile from the actual position of the pole.

Using only crude instruments, Amundsen and his men came within one mile of the actual position of the South Pole.

Members of Scott's ill-fated expedition to the South Pole, including Scott himself (standing center), reached the South Pole in 1912 but died on the return journey.

Weak, starving, cold, and pinned down by the blizzard, the three men died soon after Scott had finished writing his final words.

"Loyal to the Last"

When the news of his death reached Britain, Scott became a folk hero. There was something brave and noble about his demise: The image of the men stoically awaiting their deaths in the midst of a pounding blizzard struck a chord, and not only in England. It was tragic, and yet at the same time grand, that Scott had given his life for science and sacrificed himself in the quest for a great goal. As a contemporary biographer put it, Scott's death demonstrated

that "men can still be found to face hardship and even death in pursuit of an idea . . . loyal to the last to the charge they have undertaken."[65]

The truth was more complex. In part, of course, the travelers were indeed killed by poor weather conditions. But much of the blame for the tragedy must rest with Scott. As during his previous expedition, there was plenty to criticize about his leadership. His decision to lug rocks home from the pole slowed the men down and contributed to their deaths. Likewise, though he had originally intended to bring three companions on the final push to the pole, he added a fourth at the last minute, thereby stretching the already thin rations to the breaking point. Once again, too, Scott underestimated how much food the men would need, and his refusal to use dogs also led to the disaster.

Still, Scott's mistakes were not the entire story of his expedition. Despite the deaths of Scott and the four explorers with him, other members of his expedition had gone off in different directions and brought back valuable information about the Antarctic. Most notably, three

of his men made an important winter trek along the coastline to observe emperor penguins as they nested. The explorers returned with penguin eggs, notebooks full of observations, and a more thorough mapping of the region's coastline than ever before.

Scott's own journey south ultimately added to the world's understanding of Antarctica, too. The following spring,

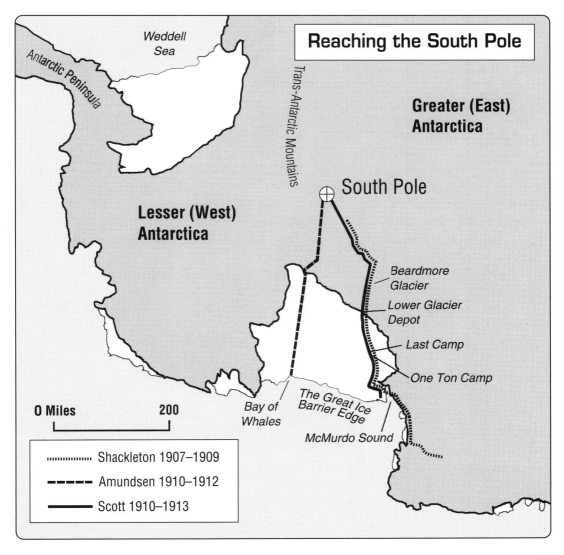

Reaching the South Pole

Weddell Sea

Antarctic Peninsula

Trans-Antarctic Mountains

Greater (East) Antarctica

Lesser (West) Antarctica

South Pole

Beardmore Glacier

Lower Glacier Depot

Last Camp

One Ton Camp

0 Miles 200

Bay of Whales

The Great Ice Barrier Edge

McMurdo Sound

··········· Shackleton 1907–1909

----- Amundsen 1910–1912

——— Scott 1910–1913

members of his expedition traveled inland to see if they could determine what had happened to Scott and his companions. They found the frozen bodies of the last three explorers in the tent where the men had died. They also found Scott's journals, which described the men's route down to the pole and back, and several informative letters as well. All these sources helped provide a fuller picture of the geography, weather, and geology of the Antarctic Continent.

Explorers and the Truth

The typical explorer is intensely single-minded. Most adventurers leave behind spouses, parents, and children; most put job and career plans on hold while they pursue their dream. Before heading out, they have spent years poring over maps, researching weather conditions, and dreaming of returning home to applause, glory, and even adulation. Over the years, a good portion of their personal identity becomes wrapped up in achieving whatever goal they have set for themselves—whether climbing Mount Everest, discovering the source of the Amazon, or finding the South Pole.

But not all explorers reach their goals. Poor weather conditions, insufficient food, ill companions—all can conspire to drive explorers home before achieving success. That can be embarrassing, even humiliating. Under the circumstances, it is sometimes tempting for explorers to lie about their progress: to add an extra hundred miles to a cross-country trek, another thousand feet to an ascent up a rock face, a few more days to a journey that ended too soon. That is especially true if the explorer is trying to reach a place no one has ever visited before; who, after all, is to contradict his or her story?

In some instances, explorers have done exactly this. Most notable, perhaps, is the story of Frederick Cook, the surgeon aboard Adrien de Gerlache's ship when it was stuck in the Antarctic pack ice. In 1909 Cook claimed to have visited the North Pole. In reality, however, the observations he made in his journals bore little resemblance to actual conditions on the way to the pole. Although a few people today accept his story as true, most agree that Cook simply lied. Similar charges have been levied against Robert Peary, whose North Pole claims are considerably stronger than Cook's but are subject to some of the same concerns.

However, there is no evidence that any Antarctic explorer has done the same. Charles Wilkes said he saw land that did not actually exist, but most historians believe this to have been an honest mistake. Shackleton never claimed to have reached the pole; Bellingshausen never claimed to have seen the Antarctic Continent. At the same time, physical evidence demonstrates that both Scott and Amundsen did reach the pole, just as they said they did. On the whole, Antarctic explorers have been an unusually honest lot.

There was one important footnote, too. The explorers hauled Scott's polar rock samples back to McMurdo Sound and from there to Europe. The weight of the rocks had clearly helped doom Scott and his men, and several of his fellow explorers wished aloud that the men had dumped the samples early in their return trip. But in fact, the rocks proved quite valuable. Once analyzed, they helped geologists determine the approximate age of that part of Antarctica and make informed guesses about the continent's origin.

Amundsen and Antarctica

Amundsen's expedition, in the meantime, would prove extremely controversial. Many people, especially in England, resented the Norwegian's achievements. They thought the pole should have been Scott's to discover; if not Scott's, then some other British explorer's. Certainly it was true that British explorers, from Cook and Ross to Shackleton and Scott, had done important work in the Antarctic; and it was likewise true that the only previous voyages into the interior had been carried out by Englishmen. Still, Amundsen had pioneered a new route to the pole; he had not simply copied Scott's plans. And he and his backers flatly rejected the idea that the pole was the property of any one explorer or nation.

Amundsen's methods stirred up other concerns, too. His use of dogs struck some, again especially in England, as not quite fair. Scott's distaste for sled dogs had rubbed off on the English public. It seemed to them more noble and pure to rely on the power and will of humans alone. Amundsen's initial secrecy about going south also seemed less than honorable. And some observers dismissed Amundsen as a mere adventurer. In comparison with Scott, Shackleton, or Drygalski, Amundsen had done no scientific work on this voyage. He had returned to Europe with no prizes other than the discovery of the pole.

But even if finding the South Pole was all Amundsen had done, that was enough. Reaching the pole was no trivial achievement. That was especially true given the grace and ease with which Amundsen had accomplished his goal. The pole, after all, had been at the center of the dreams and goals of generations of explorers. And Amundsen had found it.

Besides, Amundsen had not simply reached the pole. He had charted and mapped a large and previously unknown portion of Antarctica. He had pioneered a way into the continent's interior, discovered a new glacier, and found a mountain range. He and his companions hacked and pulled their way up a steep and icy mountain slope, working in subzero conditions while wrestling a ton of supplies up alongside them. Perhaps Amundsen should have been more honest about his intentions, but in the end, he had done as much as any other explorer to fill in the blank spots on the map of Antarctica.

CONCLUSION

The Era of Science

Just sixteen years elapsed between Leonard Kristensen's landing at Cape Adare in 1895 and Amundsen's arrival at the South Pole in 1911. But those sixteen years had been extraordinarily eventful. In that time, explorers had learned a great deal about the Antarctic, from traversing the polar plateau to understanding how to winter safely on the continent, from exploring the glaciers at the edge of the Ross Ice Shelf to learning how to undertake a sledge journey across the sea ice. As a result, human knowledge of Antarctica's geography had taken an enormous leap.

To be sure, the discovery of the South Pole did not signal the end of Antarctic exploration. Large sections of the coastline had been mapped, but even larger sections had not. While the eastern half of the Ross Sea south of New Zealand had been thoroughly charted, for instance, the Weddell Sea on the other side of the continent had scarcely been investigated at all. The two known routes to the South Pole began and ended within a few dozen miles of one another. Most of the rest of the interior, moreover, remained a mystery.

In the next few decades, several new expeditions set out to learn more about Antarctica. The first of these used ships, sledges, and other methods of travel similar to those of Scott and Amundsen. Douglas Mawson, the Australian geologist who had accompanied Shackleton, explored the western edge of the Ross Sea between 1911 and 1914. Shackleton himself returned to the Antarctic in 1914 aboard the ship *Endurance*. When his ship was unexpectedly caught in sea ice, however, he was unable to carry out the journey he had planned. Instead of becoming the first to cross the continent, he became known for a daring and dramatic escape from the clutches of the ice.

But the journeys of Mawson and Shackleton marked the end of an era. The world was changing, and Antarctic exploration was changing, too. For many years, nearly every journey toward Antarctica had combined drama, adventure, and new geographical knowledge. The explorers who had ventured to this distant and forbidding part of the world had been eager to test their mettle against the forces of nature; they had welcomed the challenge of not simply finding new mountains, coasts, and continents, but of surviving in some of the harshest conditions the world had to offer.

After 1920 that was no longer the case. Events in the years following the discovery of the South Pole changed exploration of Antarctica for good. A new breed of explorer quickly took the place of the earlier adventurers. As journalist and environmentalist John May puts it, "By 1920 the Golden Age of Antarctic exploration was over. There would be other expeditions but none would carry with them the

A pack of sled dogs sits as Ernest Shackleton's ship, the Endurance, *sinks in the Weddell Sea. Shackleton returned to Antarctica in 1914 to attempt the first crossing of the continent.*

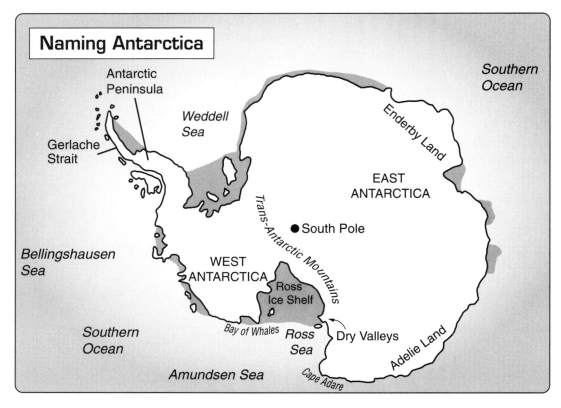

Naming Antarctica

Antarctic Peninsula

Southern Ocean

Weddell Sea

Gerlache Strait

Enderby Land

EAST ANTARCTICA

● South Pole

Bellingshausen Sea

Trans-Antarctic Mountains

WEST ANTARCTICA

Ross Ice Shelf

Southern Ocean

Bay of Whales

Ross Sea

Dry Valleys

Adelie Land

Amundsen Sea

Cape Adare

same power and glamour. The unknown had been reduced and the scientist became the key figure in the new era of Antarctic history."[66]

May's statement is not an exaggeration. Since 1920 the importance of science and scientists has loomed increasingly large in Antarctic exploration. While there had always been scientific components to Antarctic voyages, especially those of men like Drygalski, Wilkes, and Scott, science became more and more important during the twentieth century. Many twentieth-century geographical discoveries have been sparked mainly by scientists' desire to learn more about the continent's geology, biology, and climate. A 1949 expedition jointly conducted by Norway, Britain, and Sweden, for example, was dedicated to the pursuit of scientific knowledge, but made several important geographical discoveries in the process of carrying out its research.

Today, in fact, Antarctica is one of the world's great scientific laboratories. Research is carried out at bases scattered across the continent, including one at the South Pole. Some of this research concentrates on climate issues such as global warming and the earth's protective ozone layer. Other experiments focus on geology, biology, and the development of life on Earth. Much of this research is vital to our understanding of the globe and humanity's effect on it.

Antarctic Science

The science being conducted in Antarctica today includes a variety of disciplines and studies. But most Antarctic scientists carry out research projects exploring biology, geology, and climatology—the study of the weather over time.

Biologists, for instance, have made detailed studies of the habits of penguins, seals, and other Antarctic animals, along with examining the small number of plants native to the Antarctic. More globally, they have worked to understand the delicate ecosystem of Antarctica, in which the lives and health of different species are closely interrelated. Antarctica has been a valuable laboratory for biologists; with its relatively few species, the continent provides unusually clear examples of what happens when the numbers of one species are drastically reduced or increased.

Geological studies of Antarctic ice and rocks have yielded useful information, too. For example, the theory of continental drift—the idea that all continents were originally part of the same landmass—has been bolstered over the years by several important discoveries made in Antarctica. More recently, studies of fossils found on the Antarctic Continent have indicated major changes in the climate of the region over the years. Fossilized remnants of crocodiles, wood, and ancient plants, discovered in various parts of the continent, all suggest that Antarctica's weather was once mild, even tropical.

Most Antarctic scientific studies involve climate in some way, since the cold is the continent's most distinctive feature. In particular, Antarctica has served as a valuable laboratory for studying global warming. Some of the first indications of changing climatic conditions have come from research being carried out in the Antarctic. In the 1980s, for instance, scientists discovered a large hole in the ozone layer over part of Antarctica. Later, they noticed an increase in the amount of melting ice, both in the Antarctic interior and along the continent's coastline. As scientists continue to investigate the degree to which the world's climate is changing, Antarctica will remain a rich source of information for them.

Fossils such as this one of a fern found in Antarctica suggest that the continent may have once had a tropical climate.

The Growth of Technology

The growth of new technologies played a major role in making the change from traditional exploration to science. The development of reliable radios, snowmobiles, and especially airplanes enabled travelers to move around the Antarctic far more easily than before. In 1929, for instance, naval officer Richard Byrd of the United States flew to the South Pole and back from a base near Amundsen's winter quarters at the Bay of Whales. The whole trip took sixteen hours, a tiny fraction of the time spent by Amundsen and his men in making their round-trip just eighteen years before.

The ease of travel opened Antarctica to a new generation of travelers. No longer was it necessary to trudge miles across the frozen ice to observe penguin chicks or investigate a mountain. Airplanes could bring scientists and explorers where they needed to go, or at the very least close by, in a day or less. Nor was it necessary for travelers to pack in all they would need by sledge. Airplanes could shuttle in supplies and equipment for long stays on the continent. Earlier explorers were on their own once they reached the continental ice shelf, and often before; but new travelers to the Antarctic did not need to be so daring.

The impact of air travel on Antarctic exploration was undeniable. Even after the discovery of the South Pole, gaps remained on the map of Antarctica. Most of the interior had not been explored; much of the coastline was still unknown. Airplanes, however, made it much easier to investigate these missing pieces. Not only could a traveler move much more quickly in an airplane than along the ground, but it was possible to see a good deal farther from the air. "The Pole lay at the center of a limitless plain,"[67] observed Byrd, noting that earlier explorers, viewing the plateau from ground level, could only have guessed at that plain's extent.

With Byrd's flight serving as an example, Antarctic explorers increasingly took to making their journeys of discovery by plane instead of by sledge. Byrd's flight revealed little new territory, but others did. In 1935, for instance, Australian explorer John Rymill flew along the Antarctic Peninsula, demonstrating that it was attached to the rest of the continent and not a series of unconnected islands. The same year American Lincoln Ellsworth flew across the entire continent, in the process discovering several new mountains and a previously unknown stretch of land.

Other technologies proved equally important to explorers and scientists. The development of better photographic equipment allowed travelers to take photos, often from the air, and analyze them without actually spending much time in the field. Radios permitted adventurers to stay in constant contact with their home base and to summon help if that was necessary. Icebreakers allowed scientists to bring in supplies and equipment from overseas without being at the mercy of sudden freezes; enclosed snowmobiles helped protect explorers from extreme cold on short trips.

In 1929 American naval officer Robert Byrd (pictured in cockpit) became the first man to fly to the South Pole. The trip took only sixteen hours.

Filling in the Last Blanks

Piece by piece, these scientist-explorers mapped Antarctica. Surveys of the coasts and the interior, many of them completed just after World War II, added Antarctic mountain ranges, ice shelves, and coastal features to the map of the world. Lands were named, mountains measured, plateaus charted. In Scott's words, these explorers had gotten "inside that white space,"[68] and the blank areas of the map were blank no longer. By the late twentieth century, all of Antarctica had been explored—by airplane or via satellite photography, if not by human feet. With or without modern technology, it was a remarkable achievement.

But in another way, the more modern discoveries were much less critical than the explorations that culminated in the first journeys of the South Pole. The new information, valuable as it is, has mainly served to confirm the understandings and the suspicions of earlier generations of explorers. Using the materials at their disposal, for example, explorers of the early twentieth century made reasonable guesses about the size and shape of Antarctica's coastline, and further research has proved them essentially correct.

Similarly, modern explorers have proved that Antarctica is a single continent, not several adjacent landmasses divided by straits; but every Antarctic explorer since the time of James Clark Ross came to the same basic conclusion. The new ice shelves look much like the ones seen by Wilkes and Weddell; the new mountain ranges are not much different from those scaled by Shackleton and Scott.

Who Owns Antarctica?

The control of Antarctica is a complicated subject. Officially, quite a few countries claim parts of the continent. Some of these claims are based on the work of early explorers. Great Britain, for example, claims the Weddell Sea, discovered by Englishman James Weddell, and most of the Antarctic Peninsula, visited by several nineteenth-century English explorers. And France considers Adelie Land, discovered originally by Dumont d'Urville, to be a French possession.

Other claims are less reliant on exploration. New Zealand claims the Ross Sea and a long stretch of the coastline next to it. Though New Zealand did very little exploratory work, it does operate a research station in the area; more to the point, New Zealand's claims lie directly south of New Zealand itself. Chile and Argentina, likewise, had little to do with Antarctic exploration, but claim large stretches of the continent south of their own national territories. (Some of these claims overlap with those of Great Britain, as well as those of each other.)

The United States does not make any claims on Antarctica, nor does it recognize the claims of any other nations. While few other countries officially follow the U.S. lead in this matter, the truth is that most national claims today are not pressed very hard or very enthusiastically. The spirit in Antarctica today is more one of sharing than one of competition. The various research bases cooperate with one another, and coexist peacefully even when they are not actively working together. For now, at least, no one can be said to own Antarctica.

Today, research teams from nations around the world cooperate to advance our understanding of the frigid continent of Antarctica.

In detail, the map of Antarctica looks quite different from the way it looked in 1912. But in more general terms, our understanding of Antarctica has scarcely changed at all.

Antarctica Today

Today Antarctica is still a forbidding and isolated place. Yet it is a good deal less so than it used to be. Tourism has become a presence in Antarctica, with cruise ships and tours streaming in during the Antarctic summer. The great explorers of the early twentieth century would no doubt have been surprised to see this change. But they would not have been shocked to see another type of visitor: Today occasional adventurers echo Amundsen, Shackleton, and Drygalski by skiing to the South Pole, flying across the continent, or attempting similar stunts that pit themselves against the harsh conditions of the Antarctic.

Technology continues to do its share to make Antarctica accessible, too. Modems, fax machines, and video cameras have helped immeasurably in raising public awareness of the continent. Today information is instant as never before. Earlier generations had to wait months to see grainy black-and-white photos of the Antarctic region; today a camera operator with basic equipment can send real-time color videotape to televisions across the world. With a few mouse clicks, similarly, a curious student can find the present temperature on the Antarctic Peninsula or yesterday's wind chill factor at the South Pole—information simply unavailable a century ago.

And scientists, too, have helped bring Antarctica into the public's consciousness. In part, that is because of their studies. People all over the globe enjoy learning about the latest Antarctic discoveries regarding penguins, ice shelves, or volcanoes. But beyond that, scientists serve as a human presence on the most physically taxing continent in the world. Through pen-pal arrangements, newspaper and television interviews, and other methods, they can communicate to a waiting world what it feels like to spend weeks or months in one of the world's most difficult environments. For this reason, along with the explorations sparked by the thirst for scientific knowledge, it is fair to call the modern period of Antarctic exploration the era of science.

Antarctica is very much a part of the world. Modern scientists deserve much of the credit; so do government leaders, who have largely cooperated with one another in sharing resources and information about the region. But the largest share of the credit must go to the brave explorers, from Magellan and Cook down to the present, who risked their own lives in order to learn everything they could about the most inhospitable part of the earth.

Notes

Chapter One: Finding a Southern Continent

1. Quoted in Alan Gurney, *Below the Convergence.* New York: W.W. Norton, 1997, p. 17.
2. Quoted in Gurney, *Below the Convergence,* p. 138.
3. Quoted in Alan Moorehead, *The Fatal Impact.* New York: Harper and Row, 1966, p. 181.
4. Quoted in Paul Simpson-Housley, *Antarctica: Exploration, Perception, and Metaphor.* London: Routledge, 1992, p. 9.
5. Quoted in Charles R. Low, ed., *Captain Cook's Three Voyages Around the World.* London: George Routledge and Sons, n.d., pp. 178–79.
6. Quoted in Charles Neider, ed., *Antarctica.* New York: Random House, 1972, p. 36.
7. Quoted in Gurney, *Below the Convergence,* p. 138.
8. Quoted in Moorehead, *The Fatal Impact,* p. 189.
9. Quoted in Gurney, *Below the Convergence,* p. 163.
10. Quoted in Neider, *Antarctica,* p. 103.
11. Quoted in Frank Debenham, ed., *The Voyage of Captain Bellingshausen to the Antarctic Seas, vol. 2.* London: The Hakluyt Society, 1945, p. 410.
12. Quoted in Moorehead, *The Fatal Impact,* p. 188.
13. Quoted in Gurney, *Below the Convergence,* p. 181.
14. Quoted in Neider, *Antarctica,* p. 125.

Chapter Two: National Expeditions

15. Quoted in G.E. Fogg and David Smith, *The Explorations of Antarctica.* London: Cassell, 1990, p. 30.
16. Quoted in South-Pole.com, "Jules-Sebastien-Cesar Dumont d'Urville." www.south-pole.com/p0000077.htm.
17. Quoted in South-Pole.com, "Jules-Sebastien-Cesar Dumont d'Urville."
18. Quoted in Fogg and Smith, *The Explorations of Antarctica,* p. 33.
19. Quoted in South-Pole.com, "Jules-Sebastien-Cesar Dumont d'Urville."
20. Quoted in Neider, *Antarctica,* p. 139.
21. Quoted in Neider, *Antarctica,* p. 147.
22. Quoted in Neider, *Antarctica,* p. 151.
23. Quoted in Fergus Fleming, *Barrow's Boys.* New York: Atlantic Monthly Press, 1998, p. 342.
24. Quoted in Fleming, *Barrow's Boys,* p. 343.
25. Quoted in Fogg and Smith, *The Explorations of Antarctica,* p. 36.
26. Quoted in Neider, *Antarctica,* p. 173.
27. Quoted in Fleming, *Barrow's Boys,* p. 345.

28. Quoted in Fleming, *Barrow's Boys,* pp. 345–46.

Chapter Three: Living Amid the Ice

29. Fleming, *Barrow's Boys,* p. 423.
30. David E. Yelverton, *Antarctica Unveiled.* Boulder: University Press of Colorado, 2000, p. 6.
31. Quoted in Roland Huntford, *The Last Place on Earth.* New York: Atheneum, 1986, p. 60.
32. Quoted in Huntford, *The Last Place on Earth,* p. 60.
33. Quoted in Huntford, *The Last Place on Earth,* p. 69.
34. Quoted in Simpson-Housley, *Antarctica: Exploration, Perception, and Metaphor,* p. 17.
35. Quoted in Huntford, *The Last Place on Earth,* p. 74.
36. Quoted in Huntford, *The Last Place on Earth,* p. 129.
37. Quoted in South-Pole.com, "Erich von Drygalski." www.south-pole.com/p0000085.htm.

Chapter Four: Into the Interior

38. Quoted in Martin Lindsay, *The Epic of Captain Scott.* New York: G.P. Putnam's Sons, 1934, p. 32.
39. Simpson-Housley, *Antarctica: Exploration, Perception, and Metaphor,* p. 21.
40. Quoted in Huntford, *The Last Place on Earth,* p. 137.
41. Quoted in Diana Preston, *A First Rate Tragedy.* New York: Houghton Mifflin, 1998, p. 5.
42. Quoted in South-Pole.com, "Robert Falcon Scott." www.south-pole.com/p0000089.htm.
43. Quoted in T.H. Baughman, *Pilgrims on the Ice.* Lincoln: University of Nebraska Press, 1999, p. 190.
44. American Museum of Natural History, *A Brief History of Antarctic Exploration.* New York: American Museum of Natural History, 1910, p. 24.
45. Quoted in Yelverton, *Antarctica Unveiled,* p. 301.
46. Quoted in Preston, *A First Rate Tragedy,* pp. 86–87.
47. Quoted in Yelverton, *Antarctica Unveiled,* p. 338.
48. Quoted in Baughman, *Pilgrims on the Ice,* p. 105.
49. American Museum of Natural History, *A Brief History of Antarctic Exploration,* pp. 26–27.
50. Quoted in South-Pole.com, "Ernest H. Shackleton." www.south-pole.com/p0000097.htm.
51. Quoted in South-Pole.com, "Ernest H. Shackleton."
52. Quoted in Simpson-Housley, *Antarctica: Exploration, Perception, and Metaphor,* p. 24.
53. Quoted in Huntford, *The Last Place on Earth,* p. 232.

Chapter Five: The Race to the Pole

54. Quoted in Preston, *A First Rate Tragedy,* p. 101.
55. Quoted in Lindsay, *The Epic of Captain Scott,* p. 39.

56. Alan Gurney, *The Race to the White Continent*. New York: W.W. Norton, 2000, p. 282.

57. Quoted in Francis Spufford, *I May Be Some Time: Ice and the English Imagination*. New York: St. Martin's Press, 1997, p. 325.

58. Quoted in Preston, *A First Rate Tragedy*, p. 145.

59. Quoted in Huntford, *The Last Place on Earth*, p. 399.

60. Quoted in Neider, *Antarctica*, p. 204.

61. Quoted in Neider, *Antarctica*, p. 210.

62. Quoted in Huntford, *The Last Place on Earth*, p. 454.

63. Quoted in Neider, *Antarctica*, p. 228.

64. Quoted in Neider, *Antarctica*, p. 267.

65. Lindsay, *The Epic of Captain Scott*, pp. 171–72.

Conclusion: The Era of Science

66. Quoted in John May, *The Greenpeace Book of Antarctica*. New York: Doubleday, 1988, p. 114.

67. Quoted in Fogg and Smith, *The Explorations of Antarctica*, p. 61.

68. Quoted in South-Pole.com, "Robert Falcon Scott."

Chronology

1487
Bartolomeu Dias rounds Cape of Good Hope.

1519
Ferdinand Magellan leaves Spain on world circumnavigation.

1520
Magellan sails just north of Tierra del Fuego.

1521
Magellan is killed in the Philippine Islands.

1773
James Cook crosses the Antarctic Circle.

1774
Cook reaches the seventy-first parallel.

1820
Thaddeus Bellingshausen comes within thirty miles of Antarctica.

1820
Nathaniel Palmer sights the Antarctic Peninsula.

1821
John Davis and his crew visit the Antarctic Peninsula.

1823
James Weddell passes the seventy-fourth parallel.

1831
John Biscoe sights Enderby Land.

1840
Dumont d'Urville sights the Antarctic mainland.

1840
Charles Wilkes sails along fifteen hundred miles of Antarctic coast.

1841
James Clark Ross sails south to the seventy-seventh parallel.

1895
Leonard Kristensen and crew go ashore near Cape Adare.

1898
Adrien de Gerlache winters in the pack ice.

1899
Carsten Borchgrevink winters at Cape Adare.

1902
Erich von Drygalski helps establish sledging as a means of Antarctic travel.

1902
Otto Nordenskjöld escapes disaster after ice crushes his ship.

1902
Robert Scott reaches the eighty second parallel in Antarctica's interior.

1904
William Bruce visits Antarctica south of the Atlantic Ocean.

1904
Jean Charcot begins his survey of part of the Antarctic Peninsula.

1909

Edgeworth David and Douglas Mawson reach the South Magnetic Pole.

1909

Ernest Shackleton comes within one hundred miles of the South Pole.

1911

Roald Amundsen reaches the South Pole.

1912

Douglas Mawson begins his expedition to the Ross Sea.

1912

Robert Scott reaches the South Pole.

1912

Scott and four companions die while returning from the Pole.

1914

Shackleton's *Endurance* journey begins.

1929

Richard Byrd flies to the South Pole.

1935

John Rymill flies down the Antarctic Peninsula.

1935

Lincoln Ellsworth flies across Antarctica.

For Further Reading

Books

Martyn Bramwell, *Polar Exploration*. New York: DK, 1998. A short history of exploration in both the Arctic and the Antarctic. Well illustrated.

Stephen Currie, *Polar Explorers*. San Diego: Lucent Books, 2002. Biographies of five polar explorers, including Amundsen and Scott.

Philip Arthur Sauvain, *Robert Scott in the Antarctic*. Minneapolis, MN: Dillon Press, 1993. About Scott, his life, and his explorations.

Web Sites

Antarctic Connection (www.antarcticconnection.com). A commercial Web site with information about Antarctica and its history. Includes a useful time line of Antarctic exploration.

British Antarctic Survey (www.antarctica.ac.uk). Information about Britain's scientific research on and around the Antarctic continent in the past sixty years.

Cool Antarctica (www.coolantarctica.com). A look at the heroic age of Antarctic exploration, including the major expeditions of Amundsen, Mawson, Scott, and Shackleton.

Secrets of the Ice (www.secretsoftheice.org). An in-depth look at the geography of Antarctica and its importance as a scientific laboratory.

South-Pole.com (www.south-pole.com). Historical information on the Antarctic, including pages on most of the explorers mentioned in this book.

Videos

The Big Ice, prod. New Zealand National Film Unit, 39 min., Wombat Film & Video, 1984, videocassette. Focuses on the early history of scientific research in Antarctica.

Exploring Antarctica, 60 min., Questar Home Videos, videocassette. Historical accounts of the exploration of Antarctica. Includes footage from the past and present.

Works Consulted

Books

American Museum of Natural History, *A Brief History of Antarctic Exploration*. New York: American Museum of Natural History, 1910. A booklet giving the highlights of Antarctic discovery through the early 1900s.

Roald Amundsen, *The South Pole*. Vols. 1 and 2. New York: Lee Keedick, 1913. Amundsen's own description of his polar trek. Includes maps and charts.

T.H. Baughman, *Pilgrims on the Ice*. Lincoln: University of Nebraska Press, 1999. A carefully researched description of Scott's first Antarctic expedition, with reference to other voyages as well.

Richard Byrd, *Alone*. New York: G.P. Putnam's Sons, 1938. Byrd's account of a winter spent alone on the Antarctic ice.

Frank Debenham, ed., *The Voyage of Captain Bellingshausen to the Antarctic Seas*. London: The Hakluyt Society, 1945. Two volumes of Bellingshausen's records of his Antarctic journey, translated into English and carefully edited.

Fergus Fleming, *Barrow's Boys*. New York: Atlantic Monthly Press, 1998. Nicely written and informative, this book describes British voyages of discovery during the mid–nineteenth century. Among the explorers discussed is James Clark Ross.

G.E. Fogg and David Smith, *The Explorations of Antarctica*. London: Cassell, 1990. An overview of Antarctic exploration; also presents physical descriptions of Antarctica along with islands in the general area.

Alan Gurney, *Below the Convergence*. New York: W.W. Norton, 1997. The years of Antarctic exploration to 1839, the beginning of the national voyages. Detailed and informative.

————, *The Race to the White Continent*. New York: W.W. Norton, 2000. Antarctic exploration in the early years of the nineteenth century; begins where *Below the Convergence* ends.

Roland Huntford, *The Last Place on Earth*. New York: Atheneum, 1986. A thorough and well-researched history of the race to the South Pole between Robert Scott and Roald Amundsen. Huntford concludes that Amundsen was by far the better explorer and that Scott's high reputation is overblown.

Martin Lindsay, *The Epic of Captain Scott*. New York: G.P. Putnam's Sons, 1934. A short account of Scott's attempt to reach the South Pole in 1911–1912. Includes excerpts from Scott's diary and quotes about him from others.

Charles R. Low, ed., *Captain Cook's Three Voyages Around the World*. London: George Routledge and Sons, n.d. About

Cook and his expeditions. The book devotes much more space to Cook's visits to the South Pacific and elsewhere than to his Antarctic experiences.

John May, *The Greenpeace Book of Antarctica*. New York: Doubleday, 1989. A well-illustrated book about Antarctica, then and now, written from a strongly environmentalist perspective.

Alan Moorehead, *The Fatal Impact*. New York: Harper and Row, 1966. Mostly about the effect of exploration of the South Pacific, but includes useful information about the Antarctic voyages of Cook and Bellingshausen as well.

Charles Neider, ed., *Antarctica*. New York: Random House, 1972. A valuable collection of readings relating to Antarctic exploration through the years, together with brief introductory comments.

Diana Preston, *A First Rate Tragedy*. New York: Houghton Mifflin, 1998. A description and evaluation of Robert Scott's second attempt to reach the South Pole. Well written and even-handed.

Ann Savours, ed., *Edward Wilson: Diary of the Discovery Expedition*. New York: Humanities Press, 1967. Wilson accompanied Scott on both his Antarctic journeys. These are his diary entries from the first voyage, along with illustrations he drew himself.

Paul Simpson-Housley, *Antarctica: Exploration, Perception, and Metaphor*. London: Routledge, 1992. A rather academic and literary book that includes some information about the various voyages to Antarctica over the years, along with quotes from the logs and reminiscences of explorers.

Francis Spufford, *I May Be Some Time: Ice and the English Imagination*. New York: St. Martin's Press, 1997. A cultural history about British attitudes toward the polar regions in the nineteenth and early twentieth centuries. Focuses on Scott and Shackleton in particular.

David E. Yelverton, *Antarctica Unveiled*. Boulder: University Press of Colorado, 2000. About Robert Scott's first voyage to Antarctica, with information about other expeditions as well. Yelverton strives to smooth over Scott's mistakes and present him, both as a man and as an explorer, in the best possible light.

Internet Sources

South-Pole.com, "Charles Wilkes," www.south-pole.com/p0000079.htm.

———, "Douglas Mawson," www.south-pole.com/p0000099.htm.

———, "Erich von Drygalski," www.south-pole.com/p0000085.htm.

———, "Ernest H. Shackleton," www.south-pole.com/p0000097.htm.

———, "James Clark Ross," www.south-pole.com/p0000081.htm.

———, "Jules-Sebastien-Cesar Dumont d'Urville," www.south-pole.com/p0000077.htm.

———, "Roald Amundsen," www.south-pole.com/p0000101.htm.

———, "Robert Falcon Scott," www.south-pole.com/p0000089.htm.

Index

Picture Credits

Cover: © George D. Lepp/CORBIS

© Archivo Iconografico, S.A./CORBIS, 16, 22

© Bettmann/CORBIS, 29, 37, 39, 41, 53, 56, 65, 73, 78, 79, 86, 95

© Jonathan Chester/Lonely Planet Images, 72

© CORBIS, 35, 63, 67

Corel Corporation, 12, 25, 32, 45, 51, 82

© Walter Daran/Time Life Pictures/Getty Images, 11

© David Etheridge/Lonely Planet Images, 48

© Hulton Archive by Getty Images, 27, 33, 43, 55, 57, 66, 68, 85

© Hulton-Deutsch Collection/ CORBIS, 71, 76

Joseph Paris Picture Archive, 17, 19

© Wolfgang Kaehler/CORBIS, 93

© Peter Johnson/CORBIS, 40, 52

Library of Congress, 23, 81

North Wind Picture Archives, 20 (inset)

© Galen Rowell/CORBIS, 75, 96

© Joseph Sohm; Visions of America/CORBIS, 9

© Underwood & Underwood/ CORBIS, 91

© Staffan Widstrand/CORBIS, 58

About the Author

Stephen Currie is the creator of Lucent's Exploration and Discovery series. He also originated Lucent's Great Escapes series, and has published many other books and articles as well. He lives with his family in New York State. Among his interests are kayaking, bicycling, and snowshoeing—not, however, through the Antarctic.